The
SCOTTISH CLANS
& THEIR TARTANS

TWENTY-THIRD EDITION

**HISTORY OF EACH CLAN
AND FULL LIST OF SEPTS**

WARD, LOCK & COMPANY, LTD.
WARWICK HOUSE, SALISBURY SQUARE
LONDON, E.C. 4
1933

Printed in Edinburgh, Scotland

CONTENTS.

Clan Sketches in Alphabetical Order (*continued*)—

INTRODUCTION.

THE interest in matters Highland which is now so general among Scots, whether at home or abroad, brought about the preparation of the present work as a handy book of reference for all who are interested in the history of the Clans.

Prior to the adoption of surnames, which, so far as the Highlands are concerned, are of comparatively recent date, the Chiefs of the various clans were known by patronymics. A list of these patronymics is given, as in the history of the Highlands the heads of families are frequently so designated, and without a key it is difficult to understand such references.

Prefixed to each clan sketch is the badge of the clan—almost invariably an evergreen plant—and its war cry, generally the name of a prominent mountain in the clan district, or a motto associated with some gallant deed which shed lustre on the clan.

The clan sketches in the original edition were prepared by the late Mr. Henry Whyte (" Fionn "). The particulars as to the present Chiefs of clans have been carefully revised.

THE LANGUAGE OF THE GAEL.

THE native tongue of the Gael is called Gaelic. The Gaelic of Ireland, Scotland, and the Isle of Man are closely connected; indeed, till the Reformation, and for a century or more thereafter, the Irish and Scottish Gaelic had a common literary language, though the spoken tongues had diverged considerably. In the eighteenth century Scottish Gaelic broke away completely from the Irish and began a literary career of its own with a literary dialect that could be understood easily all over the Highlands and Islands. Manx is more allied to Scottish Gaelic than it is to the Irish; it is generally understood to be a remnant of the Gaelic of the Kingdom of the Isles.

Irish Gaelic is the dialect of the greatest number of Gaels, and contains almost all the old literature. It is divided into the following four leading periods:

I. OLD IRISH (O.Ir.), from about 800 to 1000 A.D. Besides some scraps of poetry and prose, we have *The Book of Armagh* (tenth century), which contains continuous Old Irish narrative.

II. EARLY IRISH (E.Ir.), from 1000 to 1200 A.D. The two great MSS. of "*Lebor na h-uidre*"—*The Book of the Dun Cow* and *The Book of Leinster*—mark this period.

III. MIDDLE IRISH (M.Ir.), from 1200 to about 1550 A.D. The chief MSS. are *The Yellow Book of Lecan*, *The Book of Ballimote*, and the "*Leabar Breac*" or *Speckled Book*, and *The Book of Lismore*.

IV. MODERN or NEW IRISH, here called Irish (Ir.), from 1550 to the present time.

The literary language of Ireland and Scotland remained the same till about 1700. The oldest document of Scottish Gaelic is *The Book of Deer*, a MS. which contains half a dozen entries in Gaelic of grants of land made to the monastery of Deer.

" The entries," says the late Dr. MacBain, " belong to the eleventh and twelfth centuries, the most important being the first—the Legend of Deer—extending to nineteen lines of continuous prose. These entries form what we call OLD GAELIC, but the language is Early Irish of an advanced or phonetically decayed kind."

The next document is *The Book of the Dean of Lismore*, an island in Argyllshire, written about 1512 in phonetic Gaelic. We call it MIDDLE GAELIC (M.G.), a term which also includes the MSS. of the MacVurich *seanachies*. " The Fearnaig MSS., written about 1688, is also phonetic in its spelling, and forms," says Dr. MacBain, " a valuable link in the chain of Scottish Gaelic phonetics from *The Book of Deer* till now." The term GAELIC (G.) means modern Gaelic.

The Gaelic alphabet consists of eighteen letters, viz., *a, b, c, d, e, f, g, h, i, l, m, n, o, p, r, s, t,* and *u.*

Scottish Gaelic printed literature dates from 1567, when John Carswell issued a translation of Knox's *Liturgy.*

There is a Chair of Celtic Languages and Literature at Edinburgh University, and a Lectureship of Celtic Languages and Literature at Glasgow University.

THE HIGHLAND DRESS

And How to Wear It.

THE Highland dress as presently worn is the result of a process of evolution. Prior to 1600 the dress of the Gaels of Ireland and Scotland was the *léine-chroich* or saffron shirt. M. Nicolay d'Arfeville, Cosmographer to the King of France, and who visited Scotland in the sixteenth century, writes: "They wear, like the Irish, a large and full shirt, coloured with saffron, and over this a garment hanging to the knee, of thick wool, after the manner of a cassock." About the beginning of the seventeenth century this saffron shirt ceased to be regarded as part of the Highland dress, and the *breacan-féile* or belted plaid and the *féile-beag* or little kilt took its place. The former was a combination of kilt and plaid, and consisted of twelve ells of tartan (six ells of double tartan) neatly plaited and fastened round the body with a belt, the lower part forming the kilt, and the other half, being fixed to the shoulder by a brooch, hung down behind and thus formed the plaid. It was possible to display considerable skill and neatness in arranging the plaits, so as to show the sett of the pattern. The *féile-beag* was made of six ells of single tartan, which, being plaited and sewn, was fixed round the waist with a strap, half a yard being left plain at each end, which crossed each other in front. This is really the modern form of that part of the Highland dress.

For everyday wear the Highland dress should consist of a kilt, jacket, and vest of tweed, or what is known as "hill checks," with horn buttons, strong *brogs* or shoes, plain knitted hose, garters, and a bonnet somewhat after the style of the "Balmoral." The sporran should be of leather, or the head of a fox, badger, or other such animal. A plaid about 4 yards long by 1½ wide, and fringed at the ends, is often worn, though of late a Highland cloak or cape has largely superseded the plaid. It is quite allowable to wear a tartan kilt with a tweed jacket and vest. The kilt should be belted round the waist, and should never be worn with braces or straps. The kilt should reach the centre of the knee-cap. The best manner of testing this is for the wearer to kneel on the ground. In this position the bottom of the kilt should just touch the ground and no more. The *sgian-dubh* is worn in the stocking, on the outer part of the right leg. The bonnet may contain a brooch showing the crest of the wearer, but for ordinary wear the less ornaments displayed the better.

In its *full dress* form, according to the best authorities, the Highland costume consists of a kilt or *féile-beag* and plaid of some regular tartan, with hose either made from the web of tartan or knitted in check of its prominent colours in the proper proportions, a doublet of cloth, velvet, or tartan with lozenge or diamond-shaped silver buttons (if an open doublet is worn, which is that usually affected by civilians, the waist-coat may be of scarlet or white or tartan), low-cut shoes, goat's hair sporran, and broad bonnet with badge and crest, a brooch to fasten the plaid, a waist belt, and a caldric or sword-belt ; the arms—a claymore or broadsword, dirk, *sgian-dubh*, a pair of pistols, and a powder-horn.

KILT.—If a member of a clan possessing one or more tartans, such as "clan," "hunting," or "dress," the person should wear his own tartan, either "clan," "hunting," or "dress," or a combination of the first two. Of course on "dress occasions" the "dress" tartan is generally worn. If belonging to a sept of any clan, he should wear the tartan of the clan of which he is a sept, if the sept has no special tartan of its own. If the sept has a special tartan, he should wear it. If not a special "dress" occasion, a person may wear a combination of his own clan tartans, such as a clan tartan kilt and a hunting tartan plaid, or *vice versa*. It is not considered proper to combine either "clan" or "hunting" tartan with "dress" tartan. If one is to wear "dress" tartan, the kilt, plaid, and hose must be uniform.

PLAID.—The long shoulder plaid should be worn, but the square shawl plaid is allowed, especially in the ballroom. The hose must correspond with either the kilt or plaid. The long plaid must be worn over the sword-belt, and removed entirely in the ballroom.

BONNET.—The bonnet should be broad and blue, somewhat akin to what is called the "Balmoral." The "Glengarry" bonnet is a modern invention, introduced about a century ago, and while "tolerated," it is not considered correct form. The bonnet should bear the crest of the wearer's clan, with motto, and also the evergreen badge of his clan or sept.

GARTERS.—The garters should be of scarlet worsted lace, about an inch in width, pattern and knot correct. There is a special knot, called in Gaelic *snaoim gartain*, or garter knot. Garters ornamented with rosettes, being a modern invention, are not considered correct.

DOUBLET.—The jacket or doublet, as already stated, may be made of velvet or cloth, or tartan cut on the bias. The jacket must be of proper Highland pattern. The oldest form is the *côta-geàrr*, something like what is commonly called a "swallow-tail," but cut short in the tails, or even like an ordinary shooting coat, but short, and with Highland pocket flaps and cuffs. The buttons must be lozenge or diamond-shaped. The buttoned-up doublet is allied to the military, while the open doublet is favoured by civilians.

SPORRAN.—A sporran of goat skin—black, grey, or white—with or without tassels, but considered more complete with tassels. The mounting of the sporran should show the crest of the clan, with motto, and the ornamentations thereon should be Celtic in design, and correspond with those on the brooch, belt, and buckles.

SHOES.—The shoes must be low cut. Buckles are generally allowed; when such are worn, they must be uniform in ornament with the belts, buckles, etc.

BELTS.—Sword-belt, etc., of black leather, bearing crest; buckles to be ornamented.

CLAYMORE, ETC.—A double-channelled blade with basket hilt, lined with scarlet cloth or tartan to correspond with the dress. Dirk of proper pattern, and bearing uniform Celtic ornamentations. *Sgian-dubh* of proper pattern, uniform with dirk in design.

PISTOL, ETC.—The proper pistol is a single-barrelled muzzle-loading belt pistol of antique pattern, having the ramrod attached to the barrel. Powder-horn worn on the right side, with the mouthpiece to the front.

ORNAMENTS.—The ornaments should be embossed, etched

or engraved. They consist of buckles for shoes and belts; a mounting for the sporran, on which is displayed the proper crest, which should also appear on the waist- and sword-belts; an ornament for the bonnet, on which is shown the proper crest and motto; and a brooch to fasten the plaid, with or without a cairngorm or other stone, and ornamented uniformly with the buckles, etc.

GENERAL.—The whole dress should appear to be uniform— the arms and ornaments all being of the same degree of richness, and the design of the ornament should be similar. The wearer must carry his dress easily, "as to the manner born." Gloves form no part of the Highland dress.

Anyone not bearing a clan surname or that of any clan sept, may adopt the tartan of their mother's clan or sept should she possess a clan surname or that of a sept.

While in the past all these things have been regarded as component parts of the Highland dress, the modern tendency is to regard several of them as lingering remnants of a belligerent age, and to discard their use. Of late years it is pleasing to observe that a quieter style of dress is being adopted, and that the warlike symbols are gradually disappearing. The sword, pistol, and powder-horn are no longer considered necessary parts of the dress, and the "ornaments" are more subdued. Competitions for the "best dressed Highlander" are dying out, and the picturesque dress of the Gael is being worn in graceful simplicity.

HIGHLAND PERSONAL NAMES AND SURNAMES.

Abbreviations.—Ag.S., Anglo-Saxon; Eng., English; G., Gaelic; M.G., Middle Gaelic; O.G., Old Gaelic; Gr., Greek; Heb., Hebrew; Ir., Irish; E.Ir., Early Irish; M.Ir., Middle Irish; O.Ir., Old Irish; Lat., Latin; Fr., French; Ger., German; N., Norse; Sc., Scotch.[1]

ADAM, G. **Adhamh,** from Heb. *Adam,* red.   Hence MacAdam and MacCadie.

ADAMNAN, G. **Adhmhnan** (pronounced *yownan* or *yónan*), "little Adam," a Gaelic diminutive from Adam.

ALEXANDER, G. **Alasdair ;** Sc. Sandy, from Gr. "helper of men."   Hence G. **MacAlasdair,** MacAlister; further Mac-andie (*from Sandy*).

ALLAN, G. **Ailean,** from G. *al,* a rock.   Hence MacAllan.

ALPIN, G. **Ailpein,** from Pictish or Welsh sources; probably from Latin *Albinus,* from *albus,* white.   Hence G. **Mac-Ailpein,** MacAlpine.

ANDREW, G. **Aindrea, Gilleanndrais ;** Eng. Gillanders, "St. Andrew's *gille,*" from Gr. "man."   Hence Mac-Andrew, Gillanders, and Anderson.

ANGUS, G. **Aonghas,** "unique choice."   Hence G. **Mac-Aonghais,** Macinnes.

ARCHIBALD, G. **Gilleasbuig,** "Bishop's *gille.*"   Hence Gillespie.   The name Archibald has no apparent connection with Gillespie in meaning or origin.

---

[1] For an explanation of the periods referred to see Chapter on " The Language of the Gael," page 9.

ARTHUR, G. **Artair**, O.Ir., *Art*; Celtic origin, " high." Hence G. **MacArtair**, MacArthur.

BAIN, from G. *bàn*, white. Hence G. **MacGillebhàin**, " Fair *gille*," rendered into Eng. by Whyte; whence also Mac-Gilvane.

BARTHOLOMEW, G. **Parlan**; Ir. *Parthalon*, " Son of Furrows." Hence Clan MacFarlane, G. **MacPhàrlain**.

BROWN, G. **Mac-a'-Bhriuthainn**; Ger. *bruno*, brown. May also be from G. *britheamh*, a judge. Hence Mac-brayne.

CAMERON, G. **Camshron, Camran**, from *cam*, wry, and *sròn*, nose—" wry nose." Cf. *Caimbeul* for Campbell.

CAMPBELL, G. **Caimbeul**, from *cam*, wry, and *beul*, mouth—" wry mouth."

CARMICHAEL, G. **MacGillemhicheil**, " Son of the *gille* of St. Michael." The name Carmichael is from the place-name in Lanark, meaning the " Seat of St. Michael."

CATTANACH, CHATTAN, G. **Catanach**, " belonging to Clan Chattan "—who claim descent from *Gille-Catan*, " Servant of St. Catan."

CHARLES, G. **Teàrlach**; in origin same as Sc. *carle*, and meaning " man." Hence *MacKerlie*, Sc. Charlie.

CHISHOLM, G. **Siosal, Siosalach**, a Border name from the place-name Chisholm, Roxburghshire.

CHRISTOPHER. *See* Gilchrist.

CLARK, G. **Cléireach**, from G. *cléireach*, a clerk or cleric; also G. **Mac-a'-Chléirich**. Hence MacChlery.

COLL, G. **Colla**, " high." Hence MacColl.

COLIN, G. **Cailean**, evidently a dialectic form from *cuilean*, whelp. A personal name long associated with the Campbells, whose Chief is *MacCailein Mór*.

COWAN. *See* MacCowan.

CRERAR, G. **Criathrar**, a Loch Tayside name, from " riddler "—G. *criathar*, to riddle.

CUMMING, G. **Cuimein, Cuimeanach**; Eng. Comyn, a Norman family, doubtless a territorial designation.

DAVID, G. **Daibhidh**, in common speech **Dàidh**. Hence **Clann Dàidh**, the Davidsons.

DERMID, G. **Diarmad**; Ir. *Dermit, Dermot,* "freeman." The Campbells are known as *Siol Diarmad*—descendants of Dermid, of classic fame.

DEWAR, G. **Deòir, Deòireach,** from G. *deòradh,* a pilgrim. Hence Macindeor.

DONALD, G. **Dòmhnull,** "world-ruler." Hence MacDonald.

DUFF, M.Ir. **Dubh** (*Clann Dubh,* Clan Duff). Hence MacDuff. The family name Duff is merely the adjective *dubh* used epithetically. See Macphee.

DUFFY. See Macphee.

DUGALD, G. **Dùghall**; M.Ir. *Dubgall,* "Black Stranger." Hence **MacDhùghaill,** MacDougall, and MacDowell.

DUNCAN, G. **Donnchadh,** from *donn,* brown, *cath,* a battle— "Brown Warrior."

EDWARD, G. **Éideard, Imhear, Iomhar.** The first is the English Edward, borrowed; the second is the Norse *Ivarr,* borrowed. See MacIver.

EVANDER. See MacIver.

EWEN, G. **Eóghan,** "well born, good." Hence MacEwen. See Hugh.

FARQUHAR, G. **Fearchar,** "super-dear one." Hence **Mac-Fhearchair,** MacErchar, Farquharson, MacFarquhar.

FERGUS, G. **Fearghas,** "super-choice." Hence **MacFhear-ghais,** Ferguson, MacKerras.

FINGAL, G. **Fionn,** Macpherson's **Fionnghal.** See *Fionnaghal,* the Gaelic form of Flora.

FINLAY, G. **Fionnla, Fionnlagh,** "fair hero." Hence Finlayson, Mackinlay (**MacFhionnlaigh**).

FORBES, G. **Foirbeis Foirbeiseach,** from the place-name *Forbes,* in Aberdeenshire; also called G. *Clann Mhorguinn.* See Morgan.

FRASER, G. **Friseal, Frisealach,** usually referred to O.Fr. *freze,* a strawberry. Strawberry leaves form part of the Fraser armorial bearings.

GALBRAITH, G. **Mac-a'-Bhreatnaich,** "Son of the Briton" (of Strathclyde).

GEORGE, G. **Seòras, Seòrsa, Deòrsa,** from Gr. "a farmer" or "worker of the earth." Hence MacGeorge.

GILBERT, G. **Gilleabart, Gillebride.** Gilbert is from Ag.S. *Gislebert,* "bright hostage"; **Gillebride** is St. Bridget's slave or *gille.*

GILCHRIST, G. **Gillecriosd,** "Servant of Christ." Hence MacGilchrist. It is also rendered Christopher.

GILLESPIE, G. **Gilleasbuig.** *See* Archibald.

GILLIES, G. **Gilliosa,** "Servant of Jesus." From **Mac-'ill-Ios'** comes the English form Lees, MacLeish.

GLASS, G. **Glas,** "grey." Hence Macglashan.

GODFREY, G. **Goraidh ;** Ag.S. *Godefrid,* "God's peace."

GORDON, G. **Gòrdan, Gòrdon, Gòrdonach,** from the parish name of *Gordon.*

GOW, G. **Gobha,** "a smith." Hence MacGowan.

GRANT, G. **Grannd.** Originally Englished from "grand."

GREGOR, G. **Griogair, Griogarach,** from Lat. *Gregorius,* "watchman." Hence **MacGriogair,** MacGregor, Gregory.

GUNN, G. **Guinne, Gunnach ;** N. *gunnr,* war.

HAROLD, G. **Harailt,** from N. *Haraldr,* herald. Hence Macraild.

HECTOR, G. **Eachunn,** "horse lord or horseman." Hence MacEchen.

HENRY, G. **Eanruig,** from O.Eng. Henrie, "home ruler." Hence MacKendrick, Henderson.

HUGH, G. **Uisdean, Huisdean,** in Argyll *Eóghan.*

JAMES, G. **Seumas,** from the Eng. James, a modification of Heb. *Jacob,* supplanter ; Sc. Jamie. Hence Jamieson.

JOHN, G. **Iain,** older **Eòin,** "The Lord's Grace." Hence **MacIain,** MacKain, Johnston.

KATHEL, G. **Cathal.** Hence **MacCathail,** MacCall, Mac-Kail.

KENNEDY, G. **Ceannaideach, Ceanadaidh ;** E.Ir. *Cennetich,* "ugly head." Called also **MacUalraig** or **MacUaraig,** from Walrick Kennedy (sixteenth century), who first settled in Lochaber. Sometimes written **MacCuaraig.**

KENNETH, G. **Coinneach,** " fire-sprung." Hence **MacCoinnich,** MacKenzie ; Sc. Kenny.

LACHLAN, G. **Lachunn, Lachlann,** from *Lochlann,* Scandinavia. Lochlann means " Fjord-land." Hence G. **MacLachainn,** MacLachlan.

LAMOND, G. **MacLaomuinn,** from N. " lawman." Hence MacClymont.

LAURENCE, G. **Labhruinn,** from Lat. *Laurentius,* St. Lawrence —Lat. *laurus,* a laurel. Hence G. **MacLabhruinn** or MacLaren.

LEWIS, G. **Luthais,** from Fr. *Louis.* Sometimes rendered Eng. Ludovick, which *see.*

LIVINGSTONE, G. **Mac-an-leigh.** *See* Macleay.

LUDOVICK, G. **Maoldònuich,** " Shaveling of the Church." Ludovick is from Ludwig, O.Ger. *Chlodwig.*

LUKE, G. **Lùcais.** Hence G. **MacLùcais,** MacLucas.

MACALISTER. *See* Alexander.

MACANDREW. *See* Andrew.

MACARTHUR. *See* Arthur.

MACASKILL, G. **MacAsgaill,** from N. *Askell* for *As-ketill,* the kettle (sacrificial vessel of the Anses or gods ; " a vessel of holiness ").

MACAULAY, G. **MacAmhlaidh,** from N. *Oláfr.*

MACBEAN, G. **MacBheathain,** from G. *Beathan,* " Life's Son." Also MacBain and MacVean.

MACBETH, G. **Macbheatha, MacBheathaig,** " Son of Life," from G. *beatha,* life. Hence MacBey, MacVey.

MACCAIG, G. **MacCaog,** from Ir. *MacTaidhg,* " Son of Teague."

MACCALLUM, G. **MacCaluim.** *See* Malcolm.

MACCODRUM, G. **MacCodrum,** from N. *Guttormr* ; Ag.S. *Guthrum,* " good or god serpent."

MACCOLL, G. **MacColla.** *See* Coll.

MACCOMBIE, G. **MacComaidh,** " Son of Tommie " or Thomas.

MACCONACHIE, G. **MacDhonnchaidh,** " Son of Duncan." The Clan Donnachie are the Robertsons of Athole, so named from Duncan de Atholia. *See* Robert.

MacCormic, G. **MacCormaig**, from E.Ir. *Cormac* or *Cormag*, charioteer.

MacCorquodale, G. **MacCòrcadail**, from N. *Thorketill*, Thor's kettle or holy vessel. *See* MacAskill.

MacCowan, G. **MacCòmhghan**, from St. *Cowan*; may also be from Sc. *cowan*, a dike-builder.

MacCrimmon, G. **MacCruimein**, from *Ruman* (on a Manx inscription); from N. *Hromundr*, "famed protector."

MacCulloch, G. **MacCullach**, "Son of the Boar"—G. *cullach*, a boar. *See* MacLulich.

MacDermid. *See* Dermid.

MacDonald. *See* Donald.

MacDuff. *See* Duff.

MacEchern, G. **MacEachairn**, "horse lord," from G. *each* and *tighearna*; also Englished Mackechnie.

MacFadyen, G. **MacPhàidein**, from G. *Pàidean*, Pat, a pet form of Patrick.

MacFarlane. *See* Bartholomew.

MacGill, G. **MacGille**, used as a curtailment. *See* Macmillan.

MacGillivray, G. **MacGillebhràth**, "Son of the Servant of Judgment," from G. *bràth*, judgment.

MacGlashan, G. **MacGlaisein, MacGilleghlais**, "The Grey Lad."

MacGowan. *See* Gow.

MacGregor. *See* Gregor.

MacHardy, G. **MacCàrdaidh**—a sept of the Farquharsons.

MacIndoer. *See* Dewar.

MacInnes. *See* Angus.

MacIntyre, G. **Mac-an-t-saoir**, "Son of the Carpenter."

MacIsaac, G. **MacIsaac**, "Son of Isaac." *See* MacKessack.

MacIver, G. **MacIamhair**, from N. *Ivarr*. *See* Edward. Also rendered Evander.

Mackay, G. **MacAoidh**, from **Aoidh**; O.G. *Æd*, fire-brand.

MacKellar, G. **MacEalair**; M.Ir. *Elair*, the Gaelic form of the Lat. *Hilarius*, borrowed. We meet with Ellar Mac-Kellar as early as 1595.

MacKessack, G. **MacCesaig** or **Mackessoc**. Also St. Kessog or Kessock.

MacKillop, G. **MacPhilip**, from Gr. "lover of horses."

Mackinlay, G. **MacFhionnlaigh**; from Finlay.

MACKINNON, G. **MacFhionghuin**, son of Fingon, "fair born"; also written Mackinven.

MACKINTOSH, G. **Mac-an-tòisich**, "The Son of the Thane," or G. *tòiseach*. Hence Tosh.

MACKIRDY, G. **MacUrardaigh**, "sea-director"; whence MacMurtrie and MacMutrie, common in Bute and Arran.

MACLACHLAN, G. **MacLachainn** or **MacLachlainn**. *See* Lachlan.

MACLAGAN, G. **MacLagain** or **MacLathagain**.

MACLAREN, G. **MacLabhruinn**. *See* Laurence.

MACLARTY, G. **MacLabhartaigh**, from G. *Flaithbheartach*; Eng. *Flaherty*, "dominion bearing."

MACLEAN, G. **MacGilleathain** for *Gill'Sheathain*, "John or *Seathan*'s Servant"; M.G. *Macgille Eòin*, "Son of the Servant of John, ' the Lord graciously gave ' "

MACLEARNAN, G. **MacGill'Ernan**, "St. Ernan's gille."

MACLEAY, G. **Mac-an-léigh**; Ir. *Donnsléibhe*. The Macleays of Lorn Englished their name as Livingstone.

MACLELLAN, G. **MacGillfhaolain**, "St. Fillan's Servant." Hence Gilfillan.

MACLENNAN, G. **MacGillfhinnein**, "Servant of St. Finnan."

MACLEOD, G. **MacLeòid**; O.G. *Léot*; Norse Sagas, *Ljótr*.

MACMAHON, G. **MacMhathain**. *See* Matheson.

MACMARTIN, G. **MacMhàirtain**, earlier *Gillemàrtain*; Eng. Martin, from Lat. *Martinus*, martial.

MACMASTER, G. **Mac-a'-Mhaighster**, "Son of the Master."

MACMICHAEL, G. **MacMhìcheil**, doubtless for *Gillemichol*. *See* Carmichael.

MACMILLAN, G. **MacMhaolain** or **MacMhaoilein, MacGille-mhaoil**, "Son of the Bald gille."

MACNAB, G. **Mac-an-Aba**, "Son of the Abbot."

MACNAIR, G. **Mac-an-Uidhir** for **Mac Iain uidhir**, "Son of the Dun (*odhar*) John." This applies to the Ross-shire MacNairs. In Perthshire and the Lennox the name is from G. *Mac-an-oighre*, "Son of the Heir," and they are regarded as a sept of Clan Farlane.

MACNAUGHTON, G. **MacNeachdain**; O.G. *Nectan*.

MACNEE, G. **MacRigh**, "Son of a King."

MACNEILL, G. **MacNèill**. *See* Neil.

MACNICOL, G. **MacNeacail**, from Lat. *Nicolas*, "conquering people." Hence Nicolson.

MacNish, G. **MacNeis,** from G. *MacNaois,* a dialectic form of *Aonghas* or Angus.

MacNiven, G. **MacGille-naoimh,** " The Saintly *gille."* Also **MacNaoimhein.**

MacPhail, G. **MacPhàil,** "Son of Paul." *See* Paul.

MacPhee, G. **Mac-a-Phì.** MacDuffie for *MacDubh-sìthe,* " Black of Peace."

MacPherson, G. **Mac-a'-Phearsain,** "Son of the Parson." The Badenoch Macphersons are known as *Clann Mhuirich.*

MacQuarrie, G. **MacGuaire;** E.Ir. *guaire,* noble.

MacQueen, G. **MacCuine** for **MacShuibhne,** from N. *Sweyn.* G. *MacSuain* now MacSwan in Skye.

MacRae, G. **MacRath,** " Son of Grace or Luck."

MacRaild. *See* Harold.

MacRanald, G. **MacRaonuill.** *See* Ranald.

MacRory, MacRury. *See* Rory.

MacTaggart, G. **Mac-an-t-Sagairt,** " Son of the Priest." Hence Haggart.

MacTavish, G. **MacThàimhs** for **MacThamhais,** " Son of Thomas," or Sc. Tammas.

MacVicar, G. **MacBhiocair,** " Son of the Vicar."

MacVurich, G. **MacMhuirich.** The bardic family claimed descent from *Muireach Albannach.* They now call themselves Macphersons.

Magnus, G. **Manus ;** Lat. *magnus,* great.

Malcolm, G. **Calum,** earlier **Gillecalum ;** Ir. *Maelcoluim,* from *maol,* bald, and *calum,* a dove—the particular *Calum* meant here being St. Columba. Hence MacCallum.

Malise, G. **Maol Iosa,** " Servant of Jesus." Hence Mellis.

Martin. *See* MacMartin.

Matheson, G. **MacMhathan, Mathanach ;** Ir. *Macmahon* " Son of the Bear." Matheson is sometimes equated with Mathew-son, G. **MacMhatha.**

Menzies, G. **Mèinn, Mèinnear, Mèinnearach,** from Fr. " of the household "—*De Meyners.*

Morgan, G. **Morgunn,** *Clann Mhorguinn* in M.G. ; is applied to the Forbeses and the Mackays.

Morrison, G. **Moireasdan,** earlier **MacGille-Mhoire,** " Mary's Servant " ; M.G. *Gillamure,* whence Gilmour. Morris is for Maurice, from the Lat. *Mauricius.*

MUNRO, G. **Rothach, Mac-an-Rothaich.** Understood to be from *Bun-roe*, the mouth of the river Roe, County Derry, Ireland.

MURDOCH, G. **Muireach, Murchadh.** The two names are from different roots. **Muireach** is "lord, king," while **Murchadh** is "sea king." From the first we have **MacMhuirich** (becoming Currie in Arran) ; from the second we have Murchison, Murchie, and Ir. Murphy. *See* Macpherson.

MURRAY, G. **Moirreach,** from the county name Moray or Murray. The Duke of Athole (Murray) is called *Am Moirreach Mór*.

MYLES, G. **Maol-Moire,** "Servant of Mary."

NEIL, G. **Niall,** "champion." Hence MacNeill, Nelson.

NICOLSON, G. **MacNeacail.** *See* MacNicol.

NORMAN, G. **Tormoid, Tormod,** from N. "Thor protection."

PATRICK, G. **Pàdruig, Pàruig** ; pet form, **Para** for *Gille-Phàdruig*. Hence MacPhatrick, Paterson.

PAUL, G. **Pòl** ; classic form **Pàl,** from Lat. *paulus*, small.

PETER, G. **Peadair,** from Lat. *petrus*, rock.

PHILIP. *See* MacKillop.

RANALD, G. **Raonull,** from N. *Rögnvaldr*, "ruler of the gods." Hence **MacRaonuill,** MacRanald.

ROBERT, G. **Raibeart, Rob,** from Ag.S. *Robert*, "bright fame." Hence Robertsons (*Clann Donnachaidh*), Mac-Robbie.

RODERICK, RORY, G. **Ruairidh,** "famed ruler."

ROSS, G. **Rosach ; Ros** from the county name Ross, from G. *ros*, a promontory.

ROY, G. **Ruadh,** red. Hence Macinroy.

SAMUEL, G. **Somhairle,** from Somerled, "summer sailor."

SHAW, G. **Seadhgh,** "strong one." *Shaw* is Englished as Seth. In Argyllshire the Shaws are called in Gaelic *Clann Mhic-gille-Sheathanaich*.

SIMON, G. **Sìm,** the personal name of Lord Lovat. Hence
  MacShimidh, "Simmie's son." Hence also Sime and
  MacKimmie.
SOMERLED. *See* Samuel.
SUTHERLAND, G. **Sutherlanach,** from the county name.

TAGGART. *See* MacTaggart.
THOMAS, G. **Tòmas, Tàmhas.** Hence MacTavish and Mac-
  Combie, also Tomason.
TORQUIL, G. **Torcull** or **Torcall,** from N. *Thorkell* and *Thor-
  ketill. See* MacCorquodale.

WHYTE, G. **MacGillebhàin,** "Son of the fair *gille.*"
WILLIAM, G. **Uilleam.** Borrowed from English. Hence
  MacWilliam.

FEMALE PERSONAL NAMES.

In Gaelic surnames the feminine equivalent of the masculine *mac*, son of, is *nic*, daughter of, and so all male *mac* surnames take *nic* when prefixed by a female personal name. "Màiri-*nic*-Dhòmhnuill" is Mary the daughter of Donald.

ANN, G. **Anna**, from Heb. "grace."
ANNABELLA, G. **Anabladh**, from Heb. "eagle heroine."

BARBARA, G. **Barbara ;** Gr. "stranger."
BESSIE, BETTY. *See* Elizabeth.
BETHIA, G. **Beathag**, "life," from G. *beatha*. Sometimes Englished Sophia.
BRIDGET, G. **Bride**, "strength."

CATHERINE, G. **Catriona ;** Gr. "pure."
CECILIA, G. **Sileas ;** Lat. "blind." Pet form Englished as *Shela.*
CHRISTINA, G. **Cairistiona ;** Gr. "Christian."
CLARA, G. **Sorcha**, "bright."

DOROTHY, G. **Diorbhàil, Diorbhorguil**, "Gift of God."

EFFIE. *See* Euphemia.
ELIZABETH, G. **Ealasaid ;** Heb. "Oath of God." Its pet forms are Bess, Bessie, Betty, Eliza.
ELLEN, G. **Eilidh ;** Gr. "light." *See* Helen.
EUPHEMIA, G. **Aoirig, Eighrig ;** M.G. *Effric. See* Effie.

FLORA, G. **Fionnaghal, Flòraidh**, "flowers"; Sc. Flory. Also G. *Finvola*, fair shouldered, G. *Fionn-ghuala.*
FRANCES, G. **Frangag**, "free."

GRACE, G. **Giorsal** ; Lat. " grace."

HELEN. *See* Ellen.

ISABELLA, G. **Iseabal,** from Heb. " Oath of God."

JANE, JEAN, G. **Sìne,** from Heb. " Grace of the Lord."
JANET, G. **Seònaid,** in Perthshire **Deònaid** ; Heb. " Grace of the Lord."
JULIA, G. **Sìleas.** *See* Cecilia.

KATE, G. **Ceit** ; Gr. " pure."

LUCY, G. **Liusaidh** ; Lat. " light."

MAGGIE. *See* Margaret, of which Maggie is a pet form.
MARGARET, G. **Mairghread, Peigi** ; Gr. " pearl."
MARION. *See* Muriel.   Heb. " bitter."
MARJORY, G. **Marsali** ;   Gr. " pearl."   Pet form May.
MARY, G. **Màiri, Moire,** or **Muire** ; Heb. " bitter."
MOLLY, G. **Malai** ;   Heb. " bitter."   Pet form of Mary.
MURIEL, G. **Muireall,** Gr. " myrrh."

RACHAEL, G. **Raoghnailt, Raonaild, Raonaid** ; from N. *Raghildr,* " God's fight."

SALLY. *See* Sarah.
SARAH, G. **Mór, Mórag,** from G. *mór,* great.   Sarah is from Heb., and means " queen."
SOPHIA, G. **Beathag** ; Gr. " wisdom."
SUSAN, G. **Siùsaidh** ; Heb. " lily."

WINIFRED, G. **Una,** " white stream.'

DESIGNATIONS OF HIGHLAND CHIEFS AND FAMILIES.

Highland Designation.	English Equivalent.
Am Mèinnearach . . .	Menzies of that Ilk.
Am Moirreach Mór . .	The Duke of Athole (Murray).
Am Drumanach Mór . .	The Earl of Perth (Drummond)
An Gleann	Ferguson of Strachur.
An Gòrdanach . . .	The Chief of the Gordons (Marquis of Huntly).
An Granntach . . .	Grant of Grant (The Earl of Seafield).
An Greumach Mór . .	The Duke of Montrose (Graham).
An Siosalach . . .	The Chisholm.
An t-Ailpeanach . . .	MacGregor of MacGregor.
Caimbeulaich bhoga Chaladair	The Campbells of Cawdor.
Chlann Theàrlaich o Buie .	Macleans of Dochgarroch and Glen Urquhart.
Cluanaigh	Cluny Macpherson of Cluny.
Donnachadh Reamhar Mac Aonghuis . . .	The progenitor of the Robertsons of Struan.
Mac-a'-Bhàirling or Mac-Pharthaloin	MacFarlane of that Ilk.
Mac-a'-Phì Cholosaidh . .	Macphee of Colonsay.
Mac-an-Aba . . .	Macnab of Macnab.
MacAdie	Ferguson of Balmacruchie.
Mac Ailein 'ic Ailein . .	MacDonald of Knoydart.
Mac-an-Lamhaich . .	Lennie of that Ilk.
Mac-an-Leistear . .	Fletcher of Achallader.
Mac-Iain-Riabhaich . .	Campbell of Ardkinglass.
Mac-an-Tòisich . . .	Mackintosh of Mackintosh.
Mac-Aoidh	Lord Reay (Chief of Clan Mackay).[1]

[1] Lord Reay is called in Gaelic *Moirear Maghrath*.

Highland Designation.	English Equivalent.
Mac-Aoidh na Ranna . .	Mackay of Rhinns (Islay).
Mac-Aoidh Abrach . .	Mackay of Strathnaver (Clan Aberigh).
MacAonghais an Dùin . .	Campbell of Dunstaffnage.
MacAonghais Cheann Loch-àluinn	Macinnes of that Ilk.
MacCailein-Mór . . .	Campbell of Argyll (Duke of Argyll).
Mac-Chailein-'ic Dhonnach-aidh	Campbell of Breadalbane (Marquis of Breadalbane).
MacAomalan . . .	Bannatyne of that Ilk.
Mac-Coinnich . . .	Earl of Seaforth (MacKenzie of Kintail).
MacDhonnachaidh . .	Campbell of Inverawe.
Mac-Cuaire (or Mac-Ghuaire)	Macquarrie of Ulva.
Mac-Dhòmnuill Duibh . .	Cameron of Lochiel.
Mac-Dhòmhnuill-nan-Eilean	MacDonald of the Isles (Lord MacDonald) and of Sleat.
Mac-Dhùgaill Lathurna .	MacDougall of Lorn.
Mac-Dhùgaill Chraignis .	Campbell of Craignish.
MacFhearghuis . . .	Ferguson of Dunfallandy.
Mac-Fhionghuin . . .	Mackinnon of Mackinnon.
Mac-Gill-onaidh . . .	Cameron of Strone.
Mac-Iain . . .	MacDonald of Glencoe.
Mac-Iain-Abrach . .	Maclean of Coll.
Mac-Iain Aird-nam-Murchan	MacDonald of Ardnamurchan.
Mac-Iain-Duibh . . .	MacAlister of Loup.
Mac - Iain - Oig, or Fear a' Ghlinne	MacDonald of Glenalladale.
Mac - Iain Stiùbhairt na h-Apunn	Stewart of Appin.
Mac-'ic-Ailein . . .	MacDonald of Clanranald.
Mac-'ic-Alastair . . .	MacDonell of Glengarry.
Mac-'ic-Artair . . .	Campbell of Strachur (MacArthur).
Mac-'ic-Dhùgaill (Mhorair) .	MacDonald of Morar.

Highland Designation.	English Equivalent.
Mac - 'ic Eachainn - Chinn-ghearr-loch	Maclean of Kingerloch.
Mac-'ic-Eóghain . . .	Maclean of Ardgour.
Mac-'ic-Fhionnlaigh . .	Farquharson of Invercauld.
Mac-'ic-Iain . . .	MacKenzie of Gairloch.
Mac-'ic-Mhurchaidh . .	MacKenzie of Achilty.
Mac-'ic-Raonuill . . .	MacDonell of Keppoch.
Mac-'ic-Bhaltair . . .	Stewart of Ardvoirlich.
Mac'ill-Eathain Dhubhart .	Maclean of that Ilk.
Mac'ill-Eathain Lochabuidhe, or Sliochd Mhurchaidh Ruaidh	Maclaine of Lochbuie, or descendants of Murdoch Roy.
Mac-'ille-Chaluim . . .	MacLeod of Raasay.
Mac-'ille-Mhoire . . .	Morrison of Lewis.
Mac-Iomhair	Campbell of Asknish.
Mac-Laomuinn . . .	Lamont of Lamont.
MacLeòid	MacLeod of Harris.
Mac - mhaoilein - mór - a' - Chnaip	Macmillan of Knap.
Mac-'ic Mhàrtainn . .	Cameron of Letterfinlay (Mac-Martin).
MacMhuirich (Cluanaigh) .	Cluny Macpherson of Cluny
MacNèill	MacNeill of Barra.
Mac-Phàdruig . . .	Grant of Glenmoriston.
Mac-Sheumais-Chataich .	Gunn of Kilearnan.
MacShimidh	Fraser of Lovat (Lord Lovat).
MacUisdein	Fraser of Culbokie.
Morair Chat . . .	The Chief of the Clan Sutherland.
Morair Ghallaobh . .	The Earl of Caithness (Sinclair).
Sliochd a' Chlaideamh Iar-uinn	The Macleans of the Ross of Mull.
Sliochd Phàra Bhig . .	The Campbells of Barcaldine and Baileveolan.
Tighearna Fólais . . .	Munro of Foulis.

A LIST OF CLAN SEPTS AND DEPENDENTS.

SHOWING THE CLANS WITH WHICH THEY ARE CONNECTED.

Sept.	*Clan.*
Abbot	Macnab.
Abbotson . . .	Do.
Abernethy . . .	Leslie.
Adam	Gordon.
Adamson . . .	Mackintosh.
Adie	Gordon.
Airlie	Ogilvie.
Alexander . . .	MacAlister, MacDonald, MacDonell of Glengarry.
Allan	MacDonald of Clanranald, MacFarlane.
Allanson . . .	Do. do.
Allardice . . .	Graham of Menteith.
Alpin	MacAlpine.
Anderson . . .	Ross.
Andrew	Do.
Angus	Macinnes.
Armstrong . . .	Armstrong.
Arthur	MacArthur (Campbell of Strachur).
Ayson	Mackintosh (Shaw).
Bain	Mackay.
Baird	Baird.
Bannatyne . . .	Campbell of Argyll, Stuart of Bute.
Bannerman . . .	Forbes.
Barclay	Barclay.
Bard	Baird.
Bartholomew . .	MacFarlane.
Baxter	Macmillan.
Bayne	Mackay

Sept.	Clan.
Bean	MacBean.
Beath	MacDonald (Clan Donald, North and South), Maclean of Duart.
Beaton	MacDonald (Clan Donald, North and South), Maclean of Duart, MacLeod of Harris.
Bell	Macmillan.
Berkeley	Barclay.
Bethune	MacDonald (Clan Donald, North and South), MacLeod of Harris.
Beton	Do. do.
Black	Lamont, MacGregor, Maclean of Duart.
Bontein, Bontine, Buntain, Bunten, Buntine	Graham of Menteith.
Bouchannane	Buchanan.
Boyd	Stewart (Royal).
Brieve	Morrison.
Brodie	Brodie.
Brown	Lamont, Macmillan.
Bruce	Bruce.
Brus	Do.
Buchan	Cumin.
Buchanan	Buchanan.
Burdon or Bourdon	Lamont.
Burnes	Campbell of Argyll.
Burns	Do.
Caddell	Campbell of Cawdor.
Caird	Sinclair.
Calder	Campbell of Cawdor.
Callum	MacLeod of Raasay.
Cambell	Campbell of Argyll.
Cameron	Cameron.
Campbell of Argyll	Campbell of Argyll.
Campbell of Breadalbane	Campbell of Breadalbane.
Campbell of Cawdor	Campbell of Cawdor.
Campbell of Loudoun	Campbell of Loudoun.
Campbell of Strachur	MacArthur.

Sept.	Clan.
Cariston . . .	Skene.
Carmichael . . .	Stewart of Appin, Stewart of Galloway.
Cattanach . . .	Macpherson.
Caw . . .	MacFarlane.
Chalmers . . .	Cameron.
Cheseholme . . .	Chisholm.
Cheyne . . .	Sutherland.
Chisholm . . .	Chisholm.
Chisholme . . .	Do.
Clark or Clarke .	Cameron, Mackintosh, Macpherson.
Clarkson . . .	Do. do.
Clergy . . .	Clergy.
Clerk . . .	Cameron, Mackintosh, Macpherson.
Clyne . . .	Sinclair.
Cockburn . . .	Cockburn.
Collier . . .	Robertson.
Colman . . .	Buchanan.
Colquhoun . . .	Colquhoun.
Colson . . .	MacDonald (Clan Donald, North and South).
Colyear . . .	Robertson.
Combich . . .	Stewart of Appin.
Combie . . .	Mackintosh.
Comrie . . .	MacGregor or MacGrigor.
Comyn . . .	Cumin.
Conacher . . .	MacDougall.
Connall . . .	MacDonald (Clan Donald, North and South).
Connell . . .	Do. do.
Conochie . . .	Campbell of Inverawe.
Coulson . . .	MacDonald (Clan Donald, North and South).
Coutts . . .	Farquharson.
Cowan . . .	Colquhoun, MacDougall.
Cranston . . .	Cranston.
Crauford . . .	Crawford.
Craufurd . . .	Do.
Crawford . . .	Do.
Crerar . . .	Mackintosh.

Sept.	Clan.
Crookshanks . . .	Stewart of Garth.
Cruickshanks . .	Do.
Culchone . . .	Colquhoun.
Cumin or Cummin .	Cumin.
Cumming . . .	Do.
Cumyn	Do.
Cunningham . . .	Cunningham.
Currie	MacDonald of Clanranald, Mac-pherson.
Dallas	Mackintosh.
Dalzell	Dalzell.
Dalziel	Do.
Darroch . . .	MacDonald (Clan Donald, North and South).
Davidson . . .	Davidson.
Davie	Do.
Davis	Do.
Davison	Do.
Dawson	Do.
Denoon	Campbell of Argyll.
Denune	Do.
Deuchar	Lindsay.
Dewar	Menzies, Macnab.
Dingwall . . .	Munro, Ross.
Dis or Dise . . .	Skene.
Doles	Mackintosh.
Donachie . . .	Robertson.
Donald	MacDonald (Clan Donald, North and South).
Donaldson . . .	Do. do.
Donillson . . .	MacDonald (of Antrim).
Donleavy . . .	Buchanan.
Donlevy	Do.
Donnellson . . .	MacDonald (of Antrim).
Dougall	MacDougall.
Douglas	Douglas.
Dove	Buchanan.
Dow	Buchanan, Davidson.
Dowall	MacDougall.
Dowe	Buchanan.

Sept.	Clan.
Dowell . . .	MacDougall.
Drummond . .	Drummond.
Duff . . .	MacDuff.
Duffie or Duffy .	Macfie.
Duilach . . .	Stewart of Garth.
Dunbar . . .	Dunbar.
Duncan . . .	Robertson.
Duncanson . .	Do.
Dundas . . .	Dundas.
Dunnachie . .	Robertson.
Dyce or Dys . .	Skene.
Edie . . .	Gordon.
Elder . . .	Mackintosh.
Elliot . . .	Elliot.
Erskine . . .	Erskine.
Esson . . .	Mackintosh (Shaw).
Ewan . . .	MacLachlan.
Ewen . . .	Do.
Ewing . . .	Do.
Farquhar . .	Farquharson.
Farquharson. .	Do.
Federith . .	Sutherland.
Fergus . . .	Ferguson.
Ferguson . .	Do.
Fergusson . .	Do.
Ferries . . .	Do.
Fersen . . .	Macpherson.
Fife . . .	MacDuff.
Findlay . .	Farquharson.
Findlayson . .	Do.
Finlay . . .	Do.
Finlayson . .	Do.
Fleming . . .	Murray.
Fletcher. . .	MacGregor.
Forbes . . .	Forbes.
Fordyce . . .	Do.
Foulis . . .	Munro.
France . . .	Stewart (Royal).
Fraser . . .	Fraser.
Frazer . . .	Do.

Sept.	Clan.
Fresell	Fraser.
Freser	Do.
Frezel or Frizel . .	Do.
Friseal	Do.
Frissell or Frizell . .	Do.
Fullarton . . .	Stuart of Bute.
Fullerton . . .	Do.
Fyfe	MacDuff.
Galbraith . . .	MacDonald (Clan Donald, North and South), MacFarlane.
Gallie	Gunn.
Garrow	Stewart (Royal).
Gaunson . . .	Gunn.
Georgeson . . .	Do.
Gibb	Buchanan.
Gibson	Do.
Gilbert	Do.
Gilbertson . . .	Do.
Gilbride	MacDonald (Clan Donald, North and South).
Gilchrist . . .	MacLachlan, Ogilvie.
Gilfillan . . .	Macnab.
Gillanders . . .	Ross.
Gillespie	Macpherson.
Gillies	Do.
Gilmore	Morrison.
Gilroy	Grant of Glenmoriston, Mac-Gillivray.
Glen	Mackintosh.
Glennie	Do.
Gordon	Gordon.
Gorrie	MacDonald (Clan Donald, North and South).
Gow	Macpherson.
Gowan	Clan Donald (North and South).
Gowrie	MacDonald (Clan Donald, North and South).
Graeme of Menteith .	Graham of Menteith.
Graeme of Montrose .	Graham of Montrose.
Graham of Menteith .	Graham of Menteith.

Sept.			Clan.
Graham of Montrose	.		Graham of Montrose.
Grahame of Menteith	.		Graham of Menteith.
Grahame of Montrose	.		Graham of Montrose.
Grant	.	. .	Grant.
Gray	.	. .	Stewart of Athole, Sutherland.
Gregor	.	. .	MacGregor.
Gregorson	.	.	Do.
Gregory	.	. .	Do.
Greig	.	. .	Do.
Greusach	.	.	Farquharson.
Grier	.	. .	MacGregor.
Grierson	.	.	Do.
Griesck	.	. .	MacFarlane.
Grigor	.	. .	MacGregor.
Gruamach	.	.	MacFarlane.
Gunn	.	. .	Gunn.
Hallyard	.	.	Skene.
Hardie	.	.	Farquharson, Mackintosh.
Hardy	.	. .	Do. do.
Harper	.	. .	Buchanan.
Harperson	.	.	Do.
Hawthorn	.	.	MacDonald (Clan Donald, North and South).
Hay	.	. .	Hay.
Henderson	.	.	Gunn, MacDonald of Glencoe (Mac-Ian).
Hendrie	.	.	MacNaughton.
Hendry	.	. .	Do.
Hewison	.	.	MacDonald (Clan Donald, North and South).
Home	.	. .	Home.
Houston	.	.	MacDonald (Clan Donald, North and South).
Howison	.	.	Do. do.
Hughson	.	.	Do. do.
Huntly	.	. .	Gordon.
Hutcheonson	.	.	MacDonald (Clan Donald, North and South).
Hutcheson	.	.	Do. do.
Hutchinson	.	.	Do. do.

Sept.			*Clan.*
Hutchison	.	.	MacDonald (Clan Donald, North and South).
Inches	.	.	Robertson.
Innes	.	.	Macinnes.
Isles	.	.	MacDonald (Clan Donald, North and South).
Jacobite	.	.	Jacobite.
Jameson	.	.	Gunn, Stuart of Bute.
Jamieson	.	.	Do. do.
Johnson	.	.	Gunn, MacDonald (MacIan), of Ardnamurchan, and of Glencoe.
Johnston	.	.	Johnstone.
Johnstone	.	.	Do.
Johnstoun	.	.	Do.
Kay	.	.	Davidson.
Kean	.	.	Gunn, MacDonald (MacIan), of Ardnamurchan, and of Glencoe.
Keene	.	.	Do. do.
Keith	.	.	Macpherson, Sutherland.
Keene	.	.	MacDonald (Clan Donald, North and South).
Kelly	.	.	Do. do.
Kendrick	.	.	MacNaughton.
Kennedy	.	.	Cameron.
Kenneth	.	.	MacKenzie.
Kennethson	.	.	Do.
Kerr	.	.	Kerr.
Kilpatrick	.	.	Colquhoun.
King	.	.	MacGregor.
Kinnell	.	.	MacDonald.
Kinnieson	.	.	MacFarlane.
Kirkpatrick	.	.	Colquhoun.
Lachlan	.	.	MacLachlan.
Lamb	.	.	Lamont.
Lambie	.	.	Do.
Lammie	.	.	Do.
Lamond	.	.	Do.
Lamondson	.	.	Do.
Lamont	.	.	Do.
Landers	.	.	Do.

Sept.				*Clan.*
Lachlan	.	.	.	MacLachlan.
Lauder	.	.	.	Lauder.
Lean	.	.	.	Maclean.
Leckie	.	.	.	MacGregor.
Lecky	.	.	.	Do.
Lees	.	.	.	Macpherson.
Lemond	.	.	.	Lamont.
Lennie or Lenny	.	.	Buchanan.
Lennox	.	.	.	MacFarlane, Stewart (Royal).
Leslie	.	.	.	Leslie.
Lewis	.	.	.	MacLeod of Lewis.
Limond	.	.	.	Lamont.
Limont	.	.	.	Do.
Lindsay	.	.	.	Lindsay.
Livingston	.	.	.	Stewart of Appin.
Livingstone	.	.	.	Do.
Lobban	.	.	.	Maclennan.
Logan	.	.	.	Do.
Loudoun	.	.	.	Campbell of Loudoun.
Love	.	.	.	Mackinnon.
Lucas	.	.	.	Lamont.
Luke	.	.	.	Do.
Lyon	.	.	.	Farquharson.
Mac a' Challies	.	.	MacDonald (Clan Donald, North and South).
Macachounich	.	.	Colquhoun.
MacAdam	.	.	.	MacGregor.
MacAdie	.	.	.	Ferguson.
MacAindra	.	.	.	MacFarlane.
MacAlaster	.	.	.	MacAlister.
Macaldonach	.	.	Buchanan.
Macalduie	.	.	.	Lamont.
MacAlester	.	.	.	MacAlister.
MacAlister	.	.	.	Do.
MacAllan	.	.	.	MacDonald of Clanranald, MacFarlane.
MacAllaster	.	.	.	MacAlister.
MacAllister	.	.	.	Do.
MacAlpin	.	.	.	MacAlpine.
MacAlpine	.	.	.	Do.

Sept.			Clan.
Macandeoir	.	.	Buchanan, Macnab.
MacAndrew	.	.	Mackintosh.
MacAngus	.	.	Macinnes.
Macara	.	.	MacGregor, Macrae.
Macaree	.	.	MacGregor.
MacArthur	.	.	MacArthur.
MacAskill	.	.	MacLeod of Lewis.
MacAslan	.	.	Buchanan.
MacAulay	.	.	MacAulay, MacLeod of Lewis.
MacAuselan	.	.	Buchanan.
MacAuslan	.	.	Do.
MacAusland	.	.	Do.
MacAuslane	.	.	Do.
MacAy	.	.	Mackintosh (Shaw).
MacBain	.	.	MacBean.
MacBaxter	.	.	Macmillan.
MacBean	.	.	MacBean.
MacBeath	.	.	MacBean, MacDonald (Clan Donald, North and South), Maclean of Duart.
MacBeolain	.	.	MacKenzie.
MacBeth	.	.	MacBean, MacDonald (Clan Donald, North and South), Maclean of Duart.
MacBheath	.	.	Do. do.
MacBrayne	.	.	MacNaughton.
MacBride	.	.	MacDonaid (Clan Donald, North and South).
MacBrieve	.	.	Morrison.
MacBurie	.	.	MacDonald of Clanranald.
MacCaa	.	.	MacFarlane.
MacCaig	.	.	Farquharson, MacLeod of Harris.
MacCainsh	.	.	Macinnes.
MacCaishe	.	.	MacDonald (Clan Donald, North and South).
MacCall	.	.	Do. do.
MacCallum	.	.	MacCallum.
MacCalman	.	.	Buchanan.
MacCalmont	.	.	Do.
MacCamie	.	.	Stuart of Bute.

Sept.			Clan.
MacCammon .	.	.	Buchanan.
MacCammond	.	.	Do.
MacCansh .	.	.	Macinnes.
MacCardney .	.	.	Farquharson, Mackintosh.
MacCartair .	.	.	Campbell of Strachur (MacArthur).
MacCarter .	.	.	Do. do.
MacCash .	.	.	MacDonald (Clan Donald, North and South).
MacCaskill .	.	.	MacLeod of Lewis.
MacCaul .	.	.	MacDonald (Clan Donald, North and South).
MacCause .	.	.	MacFarlane.
MacCaw .	.	.	MacFarlane, Stuart of Bute.
MacCay .	.	.	Mackay.
MacCeallaich .	.	.	MacDonald (Clan Donald, North and South).
MacChlerich .	.	.	Cameron, Mackintosh, Macpherson.
MacChlery .	.	.	Do. do.
MacChoiter .	.	.	MacGregor.
MacChruiter .	.	.	Buchanan.
MacCloy .	.	.	Stuart of Bute.
MacClure .	.	.	MacLeod of Harris.
MacClymont .	.	.	Lamont.
MacCodrum .	.	.	MacDonald (Clan Donald, North and South).
MacColl .	.	.	Do. do.
MacColman .	.	.	Buchanan.
MacComas .	.	.	Gunn.
MacCombe .	.	.	Mackintosh.
MacCombich .	.	.	Stewart of Appin.
MacCombie .	.	.	Mackintosh.
MacComie .	.	.	Do.
MacConacher .	.	.	MacDougall.
MacConachie .	.	.	Robertson.
MacConchy .	.	.	Mackintosh.
MacCondy .	.	.	MacFarlane.
MacConnach .	.	.	MacKenzie.
MacConnechy .	.	.	Campbell of Inverawe, Robertson.
MacConnell .	.	.	MacDonald (Clan Donald, North and South).

Sept.	Clan.
MacConochie . . .	Campbell of Inverawe, Robertson.
MacCooish . . .	MacDonald (Clan Donald, North and South).
MacCook . . .	MacDonald of Kintyre.
MacCorkill . . .	Gunn.
MacCorkindale . .	MacLeod of Lewis.
MacCorkle . . .	Gunn.
MacCormack . . .	Buchanan.
MacCormick . . .	Maclaine of Lochbuie.
MacCorquodale . .	MacLeod of Lewis.
MacCorrie . . .	Macquarrie.
MacCorry . . .	Do.
MacCoull . . .	MacDougall.
MacCowan . . .	Colquhoun.
MacCrae or MacCrea .	Macrae.
MacCrain . . .	MacDonald (Clan Donald, North and South).
MacCraw . . .	Macrae.
MacCreath . . .	Do.
MacCrie . . .	Do.
MacCrimmon . .	MacLeod of Harris.
MacCuag . . .	MacDonald of Kintyre.
MacCuaig . . .	Farquharson, MacLeod of Harris.
MacCuish . . .	MacDonald (Clan Donald, North and South).
MacCuithein . . .	Do. do.
MacCulloch . . .	MacDougall, Munro, Ross.
MacCunn . . .	Macqueen.
MacCurrach . . .	Macpherson.
MacCutchen . . .	MacDonald (Clan Donald, North and South).
MacCutcheon . . .	Do. do.
Macdade . . .	Davidson.
Macdaid . . .	Do.
MacDaniell . . .	MacDonald (Clan Donald, North and South).
MacDavid . . .	Davidson.
MacDermid . . .	Campbell of Argyll.
MacDiarmid . . .	Do. do.
MacDonachie . .	Robertson.

Sept.	Clan.
MacDonald (Clan Donald)	MacDonald.
MacDonad of Ardnamurchan	MacDonald of Ardnamurchan.
MacDonald of Clanranald	MacDonald of Clanranald.
MacDonald of the Isles and of Sleat	MacDonald of the Isles and of Sleat.
MacDonell of Glengarry	MacDonell of Glengarry.
MacDonell of Keppoch	MacDonell of Keppoch.
Macdonleavy . .	Buchanan.
MacDougall . .	MacDougall.
MacDowall . . .	Do.
MacDowell . . .	Do.
Macdrain . . .	MacDonald (Clan Donald, North and South).
MacDuff . . .	MacDuff.
MacDuffie . . .	Macfie.
MacDulothe . . .	MacDougall.
MacEachan . .	MacDonald of Clanranald.
MacEachern . .	MacDonald (Clan Donald, North and South).
MacEachin . .	MacDonald of Clanranald.
MacEachran . .	MacDonald (Clan Donald, North and South).
MacEarachar . .	Farquharson.
MacElfrish . .	MacDonald (Clan Donald, North and South).
MacElheran . . .	Do. do.
MacEoin . . .	MacFarlane.
Maceol . . .	MacNaughton.
MacErracher . .	MacFarlane.
MacEwan or MacEwen	MacEwan.
MacFadyen . .	Maclaine of Lochbuie.
MacFadzean . .	Do. do.
MacFall . . .	Mackintosh.
MacFarlan . . .	MacFarlane.
MacFarlane . .	Do.
MacFarquhar . .	Farquharson.
MacFater . . .	MacLaren.

Sept.	Clan.
MacFeat . . .	MacLaren.
MacFergus . . .	Ferguson.
Macfie or Macfee . .	Macfie.
MacGaw . . .	MacFarlane.
MacGeachie . . .	MacDonald of Clanranald.
MacGeachin . . .	Do. do.
MacGeoch . . .	MacFarlane.
Macghee . . .	Mackay.
Macghie . . .	Do.
MacGibbon . . .	Buchanan of Sallochy, Campbell of Argyll, Graham of Menteith.
MacGilbert . . .	Buchanan of Sallochy.
MacGilchrist . .	MacLachlan, Ogilvie.
MacGilledow . . .	Lamont.
MacGillegowie . .	Do.
MacGillivantic . .	MacDonell of Keppoch.
MacGillivour . .	MacGillivray.
MacGillivray . .	Do.
MacGillonie . . .	Cameron.
MacGilp . . .	MacDonell of Keppoch.
MacGilroy . . .	Grant of Glenmoriston, MacGillivray.
MacGilvernock . .	Graham of Menteith.
MacGilvra . . .	MacGillivray, Maclaine of Lochbuie.
MacGilvray . . .	MacGillivray.
Macglashan . . .	Mackintosh, Stewart of Atmole.
Macglasrich . . .	MacIvor (Campbell of Argyll), MacDonell of Keppoch.
MacGorrie . . .	MacDonald (Clan Donald, North and South), Macquarrie.
MacGorry . . .	Do. do.
MacGoun . . .	MacDonald (Clan Donald, North and South), Macpherson.
MacGowan . . .	Do. do.
MacGown . . .	Do. do.
MacGregor . . .	MacGregor.
MacGreusich . . .	Buchanan, MacFarlane.
MacGrory . . .	MacLaren.
Macgrowther . . .	MacGregor.
MacGrigor . . .	Do.

Sept.			Clan.
Macgrime	.	.	Graham of Menteith.
Macgruder	.	.	MacGregor.
Macgruer	.	.	Fraser.
Macgruther	.	.	MacGregor.
MacGuaran	.	.	Macquarrie.
MacGuffie	.	.	Macfie.
MacGuire	.	.	Macquarrie.
Machaffie	.	.	Macfie.
Machardie	.	.	Farquharson, Mackintosh.
Machardy	.	.	Do. do.
MacHarold	.	.	MacLeod of Harris.
MacHay	.	.	Mackintosh (Shaw).
MacHendrie	.	.	MacNaughton.
MacHendry	.	.	Do.
MacHenry	.	.	MacDonald (MacIan) of Glencoe.
MacHowell	.	.	MacDougall.
MacHugh	.	.	MacDonald (Clan Donald, North and South).
MacHutchen	.	.	Do. do.
MacHutcheon	.	.	Do. do.
MacIan	.	.	Gunn, MacDonald of Ardnamurchan, MacDonald of Glencoe.
Macildowie	.	.	Cameron.
Macilduy	.	.	MacGregor, Maclean of Duart.
Macilleriach	.	.	MacDonald (Clan Donald, North and South).
Macilreach	.	.	Do. do.
Macilrevie	.	.	Do. do.
Macilriach	.	.	Do. do.
Macilroy	.	.	MacGillivray, Grant of Glenmoriston.
Macilvain	.	.	MacBean.
Macilvora	.	.	Maclaine of Lochbuie.
Macilvrae	.	.	MacGillivray.
Macilvride	.	.	MacDonald (Clan Donald, North and South).
Macilwhom	.	.	Lamont.
Macilwraith	.	.	MacDonald (Clan Donald, North and South).
Macilzegowie	.	.	Lamont.

Sept.			Clan.
Macimmey	.	.	Fraser.
Macinally	.	.	Buchanan.
Macindeor	.	.	Menzies.
Macindoe	.	.	Buchanan.
Macinnes	.	.	Macinnes.
Macinroy	.	.	Robertson.
Macinstalker	.	.	MacFarlane.
Macintosh	.	.	Mackintosh.
Macintyre	.	.	Macintyre.
MacIock	.	.	MacFarlane.
MacIsaac	.	.	Campbell of Craignish, MacDonald of Clanranald.
MacIver or MacIvor	.		Campbell of Argyll, Robertson of Struan, MacKenzie.
MacJames	.	.	MacFarlane.
MacKail	.	.	Cameron.
MacKames	.	.	Gunn.
Mackay	.	.	Mackay.
MacKeachan	.	.	MacDonald of Clanranald.
MacKeamish	.	.	Gunn.
MacKean	.	.	Gunn, MacDonald of Ardnamurchan MacDonald of Glencoe.
Mackechnie	.	.	MacDonald of Clanranald.
Mackee	.	.	Mackay.
Mackeggie	.	.	Mackintosh.
MacKeith	.	.	Macpherson.
MacKellachie	.	.	MacDonald (Clan Donald, North and South).
MacKellaig	.	.	Do. do.
MacKellaigh	.	.	Do. do.
MacKellar	.	.	Campbell of Argyll.
MacKelloch	.	.	MacDonald (Clan Donald, North and South).
MacKendrick	.	.	MacNaughton.
MacKenrick	.	.	Do.
MacKenzie	.	.	MacKenzie.
MacKeochan	.	.	MacDonald of Clanranald.
MacKerchar	.	.	Farquharson.
MacKerlich	.	.	MacKenzie.
MacKerrachar	.	.	Farquharson.

Sept.	Clan.
MacKerras	Ferguson.
MacKersey	Do.
MacKessock	Campbell of Craignish, MacDonald of Clanranald.
MacKichan	MacDonald of Clanranald, MacDougall.
Mackie	Mackay.
MacKillican	Mackintosh.
MacKillop	MacDonell of Keppoch.
MacKim	Fraser.
MacKimmie	Do.
Mackindlay	Farquharson.
Mackinlay	Mackinlay.
Mackinley	Buchanan.
MacKinnell	MacDonald (Clan Donald, North and South).
Mackinney	Mackinnon.
Mackinning	Do.
Mackinnon	Do.
Mackintosh	Mackintosh.
Mackinven	Mackinnon.
MacKirdy	Stuart of Bute.
MacKissock	Campbell of Craignish, MacDonald of Clanranald.
Macknight	MacNaughton.
MacLachlan	MacLachlan.
Maclae	Stewart of Appin.
Maclagan	Robertson.
MacLaghlan	MacLachlan.
Maclaine of Lochbuie	Maclaine of Lochbuie.
MacLairish	MacDonald (Clan Donald, North and South).
MacLamond	Lamont.
MacLardie	MacDonald (Clan Donald, North and South).
MacLardy	Do. do.
MacLaren	MacLaren.
MacLarty	MacDonald (Clan Donald, North and South).
MacLauchlan	MacLachlan.

Sept.	*Clan.*
MacLaughlan . .	MacLachlan.
MacLaurin . .	MacLaren.
MacLaverty . .	MacDonald (Clan Donald, North and South).
Maclay . . .	Stewart of Appin.
Maclea or Macleay .	Do.
Maclean of Duart .	Maclean.
MacLeish . .	Macpherson.
MacLeister . .	MacGregor.
Maclennan . .	Maclennan.
MacLeod of Harris .	MacLeod of Harris.
MacLeod of Lewis .	MacLeod of Lewis.
MacLergain . .	Maclean.
Maclerie . .	Cameron, Mackintosh, Macpherson.
MacLeverty . .	MacDonald (Clan Donald, North and South).
MacLewis . .	MacLeod of Lewis, Stuart of Bute.
MacLise . .	Macpherson.
MacLiver . .	MacGregor.
MacLucas . .	Lamont, MacDougall.
MacLugash . .	MacDougall.
MacLulich . .	MacDougall, Munro, Ross.
MacLymont . .	Lamont.
MacMartin . .	Cameron.
MacMaster . .	Buchanan, Macinnes.
MacMath . .	Matheson.
MacMaurice . .	Buchanan.
MacMenzies . .	Menzies.
MacMichael . .	Stewart of Appin, Stewart of Galloway.
Macmillan . .	Macmillan.
MacMinn . .	Menzies.
MacMonies . .	Do.
MacMorran . .	Mackinnon.
MacMurchie . .	Buchanan, Clan Donald (North and South), MacKenzie.
MacMurchy . . .	Do. do.
MacMurdo . . .	Clan Donald (North and South), Macpherson.
MacMurdoch . .	Do. do.

Sept.	Clan.
MacMurray . . .	Murray.
MacMurrich . . .	MacDonald of Clanranald, Macpherson.
MacMutrie . . .	Stuart of Bute.
Macnab . . .	Macnab.
MacNachdan . .	MacNaughton.
MacNachton . . .	Do.
MacNaghten . .	Do.
MacNair . . .	MacFarlane, MacNaughton.
MacNauchton . .	MacNaughton.
MacNaughtan . .	Do.
MacNaughton . .	Do.
MacNayer . . .	Do.
MacNeal of Barra .	MacNeil of Barra.
MacNeal of Gigha .	MacNeil of Gigha.
MacNee . . .	MacGregor.
MacNeil of Barra .	MacNeil of Barra.
MacNeil of Gigha .	MacNeil of Gigha.
MacNeilage . .	MacNeil.
MacNeiledge . .	Do.
MacNeill of Barra .	MacNeil of Barra.
MacNeill of Gigha .	MacNeil of Gigha.
MacNeish . . .	MacGregor.
MacNelly . . .	MacNeil.
MacNeur . . .	MacFarlane.
MacNichol . . .	Campbell of Argyll.
MacNicol . . .	MacNicol.
MacNider . . .	MacFarlane.
MacNie . . .	MacGregor.
MacNiel of Barra .	MacNeil of Barra.
MacNiel of Gigha .	MacNeil of Gigha.
MacNish . . .	MacGregor.
MacNiter . . .	MacFarlane.
MacNiven . . .	Cumin, Mackintosh, MacNaughton.
MacNuir . . .	MacNaughton.
MacNuyer . . .	Buchanan, MacNaughton, MacFarlane.
MacOmie . . .	Mackintosh.
MacOmish . . .	Gunn.
MacOnie . . .	Cameron.

Sept.			Clan.
MacOran	.	.	Campbell of Melfort.
MacO'Shannaig	.	.	MacDonald of Kintyre.
Macoul	.	.	MacDougall.
MacOurlic	.	.	Cameron.
MacOwen	.	.	Campbell of Argyll.
Macowl	.	.	MacDougall.
MacPatrick	.	.	Lamont, MacLaren.
MacPeter	.	.	MacGregor.
MacPhail	.	.	Cameron, Mackintosh, Mackay.
MacPhater	.	.	MacLaren.
MacPhedron	.	.	MacAulay.
Macphee or Macphie	.	.	Macfie.
MacPheidiran	.	.	MacAulay.
Macpherson	.	.	Macpherson.
MacPhilip	.	.	MacDonell of Keppoch.
MacPhorich	.	.	Lamont.
MacPhun	.	.	Matheson.
Macquaire	.	.	Macquarrie.
Macquarrie	.	.	Do.
Macqueen	.	.	Macqueen.
Macquey	.	.	Mackay.
Macquhirr	.	.	Macquarrie.
Macquire	.	.	Do.
MacQuistan	.	.	MacDonald (Clan Donald, North an South).
MacQuisten	.	.	Do. do.
Macquoid	.	.	Mackay.
Macra	.	.	Macrae.
Macrach	.	.	Do.
Macrae	.	.	Do.
Macraild	.	.	MacLeod of Harris.
MacRaith	.	.	Macrae, Macilwraith, MacDonald (Clan Donald, Northa South).
MacRankin	.	.	Maclean of Coll.
MacRath	.	.	Macrae.
Macritchie	.	.	Mackintosh.
MacRob	.	.	Gunn, MacFarlane.
MacRobb	.	.	MacFarlane.
MacRobbie	.	.	Robertson.
MacRobert	.	.	Do.

Sept.				Clan.
MacRobie	.	.	.	Robertson.
MacRorie	.	.	.	MacDonald (Clan Donald, North and South).
MacRory	.	.	.	MacDonald (Clan Donald, North and South), MacLaren.
MacRuer	.	.	.	MacDonald (Clan Donald, North and South), MacLaren.
MacRurie	.	.	.	Do. do.
MacRury	.	.	.	Do. do.
MacShannachan	.	.	Do. do.
MacShimes	.	.	.	Fraser.
MacSimon	.	.	.	Do.
MacSorley	.	.	.	Cameron, MacDonald (Clan Donald, North and South), Lamont.
MacSporran	.	.	.	MacDonald (Clan Donald, North and South).
MacSuain	.	.	.	Macqueen.
MacSwan	.	.	.	Macqueen, MacDonald (Clan Donald, North and South).
MacSween	.	.	.	Macqueen.
MacSwen	.	.	.	Do.
MacSwyde	.	.	.	Do.
MacSymon	.	.	.	Fraser.
MacTaggart	.	.	.	Ross.
MacTause	.	.	.	Campbell of Argyll.
MacTavish	.	.	.	MacTavish.
MacTear	.	.	.	Ross, Macintyre.
MacThomas	.	.	.	Campbell of Argyll, Mackintosh.
MacTier	.	.	.	Ross.
MacTire	.	.	.	Do.
MacUlric	.	.	.	Cameron.
MacUre	.	.	.	Campbell of Argyll.
Macvail	.	.	.	Cameron, Mackay, Mackintosh, Macpherson.
MacVanish	.	.	.	MacKenzie.
MacVarish	.	.	.	MacDonald of Clanranald.
MacVeagh	.	.	.	Maclean of Duart.
MacVean	.	.	.	MacBean.
MacVey	.	.	.	Maclean of Duart.
MacVicar	.	.	.	MacNaughton.

Sept.	Clan.
MacVinish . . .	MacKenzie.
MacVurie . . .	MacDonald of Clanranald.
MacVurrich . . .	MacDonald of Clanranald, Macpherson.
MacWalrick . . .	Cameron.
MacWalter . . .	MacFarlane.
MacWattie . . .	Buchanan of Leny.
MacWhannell . .	MacDonald (Clan Donald, North and South).
MacWhirr . . .	Macquarrie.
MacWhirter . .	Buchanan.
MacWilliam . . .	Gunn, MacFarlane.
Macgrath . . .	Macrae.
Malcolm . . .	Malcolm.
Malcolmson . .	MacLeod of Raasay.
Malloch . . .	MacGregor.
Manson . . .	Gunn.
Martin . . .	Cameron, MacDonald (Clan Donald, North and South).
Masterson . . .	Buchanan.
Matheson . . .	Matheson.
Mathie . . .	Do.
Mathieson . . .	Do.
Maxwell . . .	Maxwell.
May . . .	MacDonald (Clan Donald, North and South).
Means . . .	Menzies.
Meikleham . . .	Lamont.
Mein or Meine .	Menzies.
Mengues . . .	Do.
Mennie . . .	Do.
Menteith . . .	Graham, Stewart (Royal).
Menzies . . .	Menzies.
Meyners . . .	Do.
Michie . . .	Forbes.
Miller . . .	MacFarlane.
Minn . . .	Menzies.
Minnus . . .	Do.
Monach . . .	MacFarlane.
Monro or Monroe .	Munro.

Sept.	Clan.
Monteith . . .	Graham, Stewart (Royal).
Monzie	Menzies.
Moray	Murray.
More	Leslie.
Morgan . . .	Mackay.
Morison	Morrison.
Morrison . . .	Do.
Mowat	Sutherland.
Munro or Munroe. .	Munro.
Murchie . . .	Buchanan, Clan Donald (North and South) MacKenzie.
Murchison . . .	Do. do.
Murdoch . . .	Clan Donald (North and South), Macpherson.
Murdoson . . .	Do. do.
Murray of Athole .	Murray of Athole.
Murray of Tullibardine	Murray of Tullibardine.
Napier	MacFarlane.
Neal	MacNeil.
Neil or Neill . .	Do.
Neilson . . .	Mackay.
Neish	MacGregor.
Nelson	Gunn.
Nicholl . . .	Macleod of Lewis.
Nicholson . . .	Do.
Nicol or Nicoll . .	Do.
Nicolson . . .	Do.
Nish	MacGregor.
Niven	Cumin, Mackintosh, MacNaughton.
Noble	Mackintosh.
Norman	MacLeod of Harris.
O'Drain . . .	MacDonald (Clan Donald, North and South).
Ogilvie	Ogilvie.
Ogilvy	Do.
Oliphant . . .	Sutherland.
O'May	MacDonald (Clan Donald, North and South).
O'Shaig	Do. do.
O'Shannachan . .	Do. do.

Sept.	Clan.
O'Shannaig . . .	MacDonald (Clan Donald, North and South).
Parlane . . .	MacFarlane.
Paterson . . .	MacLaren.
Patrick . . .	Lamont.
Paul . . .	Cameron, Mackintosh, Mackay.
Peter . . .	MacGregor.
Philipson . . .	MacDonell of Keppoch.
Pitullich . . .	MacDonald (Clan Donald, North and South).
Polson . . .	Mackay.
Purcell . . .	MacDonald (Clan Donald, North and South).
Rae . . .	Macrae.
Ramsay . . .	Ramsay.
Rankin . . .	Maclean of Coll.
Rattray . . .	Murray.
Reid . . .	Robertson of Strathloch.
Reoch . . .	Farquharson, MacDonald (Clan Donald, North and South).
Revie . . .	MacDonald (Clan Donald, North and South).
Riach . . .	Farquharson, MacDonald (Clan Donald, North and South).
Risk . . .	Buchanan.
Ritchie . . .	Mackintosh.
Rob Roy . . .	Rob Roy.
Robb . . .	MacFarlane.
Robertson . . .	Robertson.
Robison . . .	Gunn.
Robson . . .	Do.
Ronald . . .	MacDonell of Keppoch.
Ronaldson . . .	Do.
Rorison . . .	MacDonald (Clan Donald, North and South).
Rose . . .	Rose.
Ross . . .	Ross.
Roy . . .	Robertson.
Ruskin . . .	MacCalman (Buchanan).
Ruthven . . .	Ruthven.

Sept.	Clan.
Sanderson	MacDonell of Glengarry.
Sandison	Gunn.
Scott	Scott.
Shannon	MacDonald (Clan Donald, North and South).
Shaw	Mackintosh.
Sim or Sime	Fraser.
Simon	Do.
Simpson	Do.
Sinclair	Sinclair.
Skene	Skene.
Small	Murray.
Sorley	Cameron, MacDonald (Clan Donald, North and South), Lamont.
Spalding	Murray.
Spence	MacDuff.
Spens	Do.
Spittal or Spittel	Buchanan.
Sporran	MacDonald (Clan Donald, North and South).
Stalker	MacFarlane.
Stark	Robertson.
Steuart	Stewart, Royal.
Stewart of Appin	Stewart of Appin.
Stewart of Athole	Stewart of Athole.
Stewart of Galloway	Stewart of Galloway.
Stewart, Royal	Stewart, Royal.
Stuart	Do.
Stuart of Bute	Stuart of Bute.
Sutherland	Sutherland.
Swan	Macqueen.
Swanson	Gunn.
Syme	Fraser.
Symon	Do.
Taggart	Ross.
Tarrill	Mackintosh.
Tawesson	Campbell of Argyll.
Taylor	Cameron.
Thomas	Campbell of Argyll.
Thomason	Campbell of Argyll, **MacFarlane**

Sept.	Clan.
Thompson	Campbell of Argyll.
Thomson	Do.
Tolmie	MacLeod of Raasay.
Tonnochy	Robertson.
Tosh	Mackintosh.
Toshach	Do.
Toward	Lamont.
Towart	Do.
Train	MacDonald (Clan Donald, North and South).
Turner	Lamont.
Tweedie	Fraser.
Tyre	Macintyre.
Ure	Campbell of Argyll.
Urquhart	Urquhart.
Vass	Munro, Ross.
Wallace	Wallace.
Wallis	Do.
Warnebald	Cunningham.
Wass	Munro, Ross.
Watson	Buchanan.
Watt	Do.
Weaver	MacFarlane.
Weir	MacNaughton, MacFarlane.
Wemyss	MacDuff.
Whannell	MacDonald (Clan Donald, North and South).
Wharrie	Macquarrie.
White or Whyte	MacGregor, Lamont.
Williamson	Gunn, Mackay.
Wilson	Gunn.
Wright	Macintyre.
Yuill	Buchanan.
Yuille	Do.
Yule	Do.

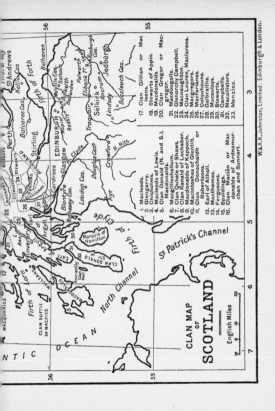

CLAN MAP
OF
SCOTLAND

English Miles

1. Macleods.
2. Macdonnells.
3. Chisholms.
4. Macleods of Lewis.
5. Clan Donald (N. and S.).
6. Macdonalds.
7. Macgillechallum.
8. Clan Quhele or Shaws.
9. Clan Ranald or Lochaber.
10. Macdonalds of Keppoch.
11. Macintoshes of Glenlitt.
12. Clan Donachaidh or Robertsons.
13. Earl of Atholl.
14. Macthomas.
15. Fergusons.
16. Clan Macian or Macdonalds of Ardnamurchan and Sunnart.

17. Clan Gillian or Maclean.
18. Stewarts of Appin.
19. Macdonalds.
20. Clan Gregor or Macgregor.
21. Macdougalls.
22. Glenorchy Campbell.
23. Macnaughton & Lochaber.
24. Clan Lauren, Maclarens.
25. Macgregors.
26. Macfarlanes.
27. Colquhouns.
28. Galbraiths.
29. Macaulays.
30. Lennox.
31. Campbells.
32. Macalisters.
33. Menzies.

W.& A.K. Johnston, Limited. Edinburgh & London.

BRODIE OF BRODIE.

THIS name is from the local place-name Brodie, Gaelic, *brothach*. The old writings of the family were mostly carried away or destroyed when Lord Lewis Gordon, afterwards (third) Marquis of Huntly, burnt Brodie House in 1645. From Malcolm, Thane of Brodie, living *temp.* King Alexander III. descended Alexander Brodie of Brodie, styled Lord Brodie as a senator of the College of Justice, born 1617, whose son and successor, James Brodie of Brodie, born 1637, married in 1659 Lady Mary Ker, daughter of William, third Earl of Lothian. Leaving nine daughters but no son, he was succeeded by his cousin, George Brodie, son of Joseph Brodie of Aslisk, and grandson of David Brodie of Brodie, brother of Lord Brodie. In 1692 he married Emily, fifth daughter of his predecessor. He died in 1716, leaving three sons and two daughters. James Brodie, the elder son and heir, died young (1720), and was succeeded by his brother, Alexander, born 1697. He was appointed Lord Lyon of Scotland 1727, and died 1754. By his wife, Mary Sleigh, he had a son, Alexander, his heir, and one daughter, Emilia. Alexander Brodie of Brodie, born 1741, died in 1750, and was succeeded by his second cousin, James Brodie, son of James Brodie of Spynie. This gentleman, Lord-Lieutenant of the county of Nairn, was born 1744, and married Lady Margaret Duff, youngest daughter of William, first Earl of Fife. He died in 1824, leaving two sons and three daughters. Their son, James, was drowned in his father's lifetime, leaving two sons and five daughters. Their eldest son, William Brodie, Esq., of Brodie, in Morayshire, Lieutenant of Nairnshire, was born in 1799, succeeded his grandfather in January 1824, married in 1838 Elizabeth, third daughter of the late Colonel Hugh Bailie, M.P. of Red Castle, and had issue—Hugh Fife Ashley, R.A., born September 1840, and died 1889.

The present head of the family is Ian Brodie of Brodie, D.S.O., born 1868, Lieutenant for Nairnshire.

The other branches of this clan are Brodie of Lethen, and Brodie of Eastbourne, Sussex, and a Brodie was made a Baronet in 1834.

A   BRODIE.

ROBERT BRUCE (King of Scotland).

THIS monarch belonged to the Norman family De Bruis, which in the person of Robert De Bruis came to England with the Conqueror in 1066. This knight received large grants of land, chiefly in Yorkshire; and his son, Robert, who was an associate of the prince who afterwards became David I. of Scotland, obtained the Lordship of Annandale. At the battle of the Standard (1138) Robert Bruce fought on the English side; while his son, the third Robert, fought under David and was taken prisoner, it is said, by his own father.

He had two sons, Robert and William. Robert, the eldest, died before 1191. William, his brother and heir, died in 1215, and was succeeded by his son, Robert de Bruce, who died in 1245. Their son, Robert de Bruce, was in 1255 nominated one of the Regents of the Kingdom of Scotland, and guardian of Alexander III. and his Queen; in 1264, with John Cumyn and John Baliol, he led a body of Scottish auxiliaries to assist King Henry III. against his rebellious barons, and was taken prisoner at the battle of Lewis with that monarch. He sat in Parliament as Lord of Annandale in 1290, and entered his claim to the Crown of Scotland, as the nearest heir of King Alexander III. King Edward I. overruled all the pleas of Bruce, and adjudged the Kingdom of Scotland to Baliol. Bruce died in 1295, aged eighty-five. His eldest son, Robert de Bruce, was born in 1245. He accompanied Edward into Scotland against Baliol. Edward had promised to raise Bruce to the throne in room of Baliol, but failed to carry out this design. Bruce retired to England and died in 1304.

By Margaret, Countess of Carrick, his wife, he left a large family. His eldest son, Robert de Bruce, born 11th July 1274, asserted his claim to the Scottish Crown and ascended the throne of his ancestors, and was crowned at Scone, 27th March 1306. After many vicissitudes, the power of King Robert I. was finally cemented by his splendid and decisive victory at Bannockburn, 1314. He died at Cardross, in Dumbartonshire, on the 7th of June 1329, aged fifty-five; he was interred in the Abbey Church of Dunfermline. His heart, after being carried to Palestine, was brought back with the body of Douglas and buried in the Monastery of Melrose.

BRUCE.

THE BUCHANANS.

War Cry :—" Clar Innis " (An island in Loch Lomond).
Badge :—Dearc bhraoileag (Bilberry) or Darag (Oak).

ABOUT the middle of the thirteenth century, Gilbert, seneschal to the Earl of Lennox, obtained from him a part of the lands of Buchanan in Stirlingshire and took his name from them. An ecclesiastical origin is claimed for the surname, as in Gaelic a Buchanan is known as *Mac-a'-Chanonaich*—the Son of the Canon—and the place-name Buchanan (*Both-chanain*) really means the canon's seat.

Donald, sixth Earl of Lennox, renewed to Maurice of Buchanan the grant conferred by a former earl on his ancestor, and the King granted a charter of confirmation to his successor of the same name.

Through marriage with a daughter of Mentieth of Ruskie, his son, Walter of Buchanan, became connected with the Royal House. The latter married the sole heiress of the ancient family of Leny. Their eldest son, Sir Alexander, distinguished himself as a soldier, and was slain in the battle of Verneuil in 1424. His second brother, Walter, succeeded to Buchanan, and his third to Leny.

Walter married Isabel, Countess of Lennox. Their eldest son, Patrick, married the heiress of Killearn and Auchreoch.

Patrick's son, Walter, married a daughter of Lord Graham. Patrick, who fell at Flodden, by his wife, a daughter of Argyll, left two sons—George, Sheriff of Dumbarton in 1561, and Walter, the founder of the House of Spittal.

By Margaret Edmondston of Dunreath, he had John, his heir, and by his second wife, Janet Cunningham of Craigends, William, founder of the now extinct line of Auchmar.

The principal line became extinct early in the eighteenth century ; and though in 1878 Mr. Francis Hamilton Buchanan established his claim as Chief, his grandson, Mr. J. H. Buchanan, died recently without issue.

The Buchanan family lands are now possessed by the Duke of Montrose.

There is a Buchanan Society in Glasgow.

BUCHANAN

THE CLAN CAMERON.

War Cry:—" Chlanna nan con thigibh a so 's gheibh sibh feòil " (" Sons of the hounds come here and get flesh ").
Badge:—Darag (Oak) or Dearca fithich (Crowberry).

THE Camerons got their surname from the *Cam-shròn* or " wry nose " of some early Chief. The first assured Chief of the clan is Donald Du (*cir.* 1411). He married an heiress of MacMartin of Letterfinlay and succeeded to her property. He left two sons—Allan, who succeeded him, and Ewen, who is generally regarded as the progenitor of the Camerons of Strone. Allan left two sons, Ewen and John.

Ewen married first a daughter of Celestine of Lochalsh. His eldest son and heir, Donald, died before his father, between the years 1536 and 1539. He married secondly, Marjory, daughter of Lachlan, second son of Malcolm Mackintosh of Mackintosh. By this lady he had Ewen, the progenitor of the family of Erracht, and John, progenitor of the Camerons of Kin-Lochiel. Ewen was succeeded by his grandson, *Eòghan Beag*—Little Ewen—who was the father of the famous Black Tailor of the Axe.

Passing over Donald and Allan, we come to the famous Sir Ewen Cameron, born in 1629. He married first, Mary, daughter of Sir James MacDonald, first Baronet of Sleat, and secondly, Isabel, daughter of Sir Lachlan Maclean of Duart, and thirdly, Jane, daughter of Colonel David Barclay (XVII.) of Urie. He died in 1719, aged ninety.

He was succeeded by his son, John, who married Isabel, daughter of Campbell of Lochnell, with issue—Donald, who succeeded, and John of Fassiefern, who died 1747 or 1748.

He was succeeded by Donald, his eldest son, known as " The Gentle Lochiel," who followed Prince Charlie and suffered with him. After Culloden he escaped to France, where he died 1748. He was succeeded in the chiefship by his son, John, who was succeeded by his brother, Charles. He died in 1776, and was succeeded by his son, Donald, a minor, who died 1832. He was succeeded by his son, Donald, who died in 1859, and was succeeded by his son, Donald, who died 1905. His son, Colonel Donald Walter Cameron, C.M.G., of Lochiel, is the twenty-fifth Chief.

There is an organisation called " The Clan Cameron," with its headquarters in Glasgow.

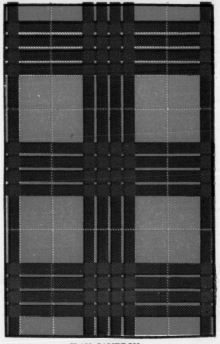

CLAN CAMERON.

CAMERON OF ERRACHT.

Badge :—Darag (Oak) or Dearca fithich (Crowberry).

THIS family were known locally as *Sliochd Eóghain 'ic Eóghain*, or "the children of Ewen, son of Ewen." The first representative of the family was Ewen Cameron, son of Ewen, by his second wife, Marjory Mackintosh.

Donald Cameron, second Laird of Erracht, was born shortly before the Rising of 1715. Some thirty years later he joined Prince Charles, and, under Lochiel, was second in command of the Camerons at the historic Glenfinnan.

After the fatal Culloden, Cameron of Erracht was for three years a homeless wanderer among the mountains. He married Marjory, daughter of Maclean of Drimnin in Morvern, and had four children, the eldest of whom was afterwards the famous Sir Allan Cameron of Erracht, K.C.B., who in 1793 raised the 79th or Cameron Highlanders. He was appointed Lieutenant-Colonel Commandant, and led the 79th through the severe campaigns of 1794-1795 in Flanders, till it embarked for the West Indies. In 1797 the battalion was broken up, and 210 joined the Black Watch.

Colonel Cameron and his officers repaired to the Highlands, and in 1798 soon raised a second 79th regiment, 780 strong. In 1804 he formed a second battalion, 800 strong. After taking part in many engagements in foreign parts, he retired from active service, and died at Fulham in 1828.

What is known as the "Erracht Cameron Tartan" was specially designed for the 79th Cameron Highlanders by Mrs. Cameron of Erracht (Allan's mother), a daughter of Ranald MacDonell of Keppoch, who, by blending the tartan of the MacDonalds with that of the Camerons, solved the difficulty which presented itself, and in this way the sentiment of both clans was respected.

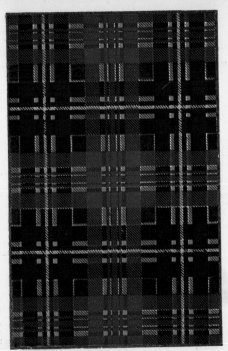

CAMERON, ERRACHT.

CAMERON OF LOCHIEL.

War Cry :—" Chlanna nan con thigibh a so 's gheibh sibh feòil " (" Sons of the hounds come here and get flesh ").
Badge :—Darag (Oak) or Dearca fithich (Crowberry).

THE original possessions of the Camerons were confined to the portion of Lochaber lying on the east side of the loch and river of Lochy, held west of the Isles as superior. The more modern possessions of the clan—Lochiel and Locharkaig—lying on the west side of these waters, were at an earlier period granted by the Island Lord to MacDonald of Clan Ranald, by whose descendants they were for many generations inhabited.

The ancient residence of Lochiel was Tor Castle, which was erected by Ewen Cameron (XIII.) of Lochiel in the beginning of the sixteenth century, and it remained the seat of the family till the time of Sir Ewen (XVII.) of Lochiel, who was born in 1629 and died in 1719, who built a mansion for himself at Achnacarry, which was the old Achnacarry burned in 1746, when the country was overrun and wasted after Culloden. Achnacarry was rebuilt early in the nineteenth century, but not completed till 1837.

The MacGillonie Camerons are generally regarded as the oldest family of the clan, while Cameron of Lochiel is designated the senior cadet. In 1492 the head of the Camerons of Lochiel is spoken of as Captain of Clan Cameron, but in 1528 the King granted a charter erecting all his land into the Barony of Lochiel, in which the Captain of the Clan is for the first time designated as "of Lochiel." After this the Chief is "of Lochiel."

The following is a description of the Arms of the Chief: Gules, two bars or. *Crest*—a sheaf of five arrows proper, tied with a band gules. *Motto*—"Unite." On a compartment below the shield, on which are these words " *Pro Rege et Patria*," are placed for *Supporters* two savages wreathed about the heads and middles with oak branches proper, each holding in his exterior hand a Lochaber axe of the last.

CAMERON, LOCHIEL.

THE CAMPBELLS OF ARGYLL.

War Cry :—" Cruachan " (A mountain near Loch Awe).
Badge :—Roid (Wild Myrtle) or Garbhag an t-sléibhe
(Fir Club Moss).

THE real founder of the family of Argyll was *Cailean Mór*,
from whom the Chief gets his patronymic of *MacCailean
Mór*. This Colin was slain at *Ath-Dearg* (Red Ford), in
Lorn, 1294.

Sir Colin Campbell (*Cailean Iongantach*) succeeded his
father, Sir Archibald, who died in 1372. He died in 1413,
and was succeeded by his son, Sir Duncan, who was created
Lord Campbell, and was the first of the family that took the
title of Argyll. He died in 1453.

Archibald Roy succeeded his father, and was succeeded by
his son, Colin, who was created Earl of Argyll in 1457. He
died in 1493, and was succeeded by his son, Archibald, second
Earl of Argyll, who fell at Flodden. He was succeeded by his
son, Colin, third Earl of Argyll. Archibald, his son, succeeded
him. He died in 1558, and was succeeded by his son, Archibald, who died without issue in 1575, and was succeeded by his
brother, Colin, sixth Earl of Argyll. Archibald, seventh Earl,
reduced the MacGregors in 1603. He was succeeded by Archibald, his son, in 1638 as eighth Earl. He was created Marquis
of Argyll in 1641. He was beheaded in 1661. His estates,
after being forfeited, were restored to his son, Archibald, with
the title of Earl of Argyll. For the part he took in the Monmouth rebellion he was beheaded in 1685. He was succeeded
by his son, Archibald, tenth Earl, who was created a Duke in
1701. He died in 1703, and was succeeded by his son, John,
second Duke of Argyll and Earl of Greenwich. He died 1743.
He was succeeded by his brother, Archibald, third Duke, who
died 1761. Being without issue, the title devolved on his
cousin, General John Campbell of Mamore. He died in 1770,
and was succeeded by his son, John, fifth Duke, who died 1790.
He left two sons—George, sixth Duke, who died 1839 ; and
John, seventh Duke, who died in 1847, leaving George, eighth
Duke, who died 1900. He was thrice married, and by his first
wife had issue five sons and seven daughters. He was succeeded by his eldest son, John George Edward Henry Douglas
Sutherland, born 1845, who married Princess Louise in 1871.
His nephew, Sir Niall Diarmid Campbell, became tenth Duke
in 1914.

CAMPBELL, ARGYLL.

THE CAMPBELLS OF BREADALBANE.

War Cry :—" Cruachan " (A mountain near Loch Awe).
Badge :—Roid (Wild Myrtle) or Garbhag an t-sléibhe
(Fir Club Moss).

AFTER the House of Argyll, the leading family are the
Campbells of Breadalbane, whose ancestor was Black
Colin of Rome, second son of Sir Duncan Campbell,
Knight of Loch Awe, by his wife, Lady Marjory Stewart. This
accounts for the patronymic of the House of Breadalbane—
Mac-Chailein-Mhic-Dhonnachaidh (son of Colin son of Duncan).
In 1432 Sir Colin received as patrimony from his father the lands
of Glenorchy, from which the MacGregors had been
driven.

Sir Colin was married four times. First to Mary, daughter
of Duncan, Earl of Lennox, and then to Lady Margaret Stewart,
co-heiress of John Stewart, Lord of Lorn, with her he received
the third of the lands of Lorn. Sir Colin died in 1498.

The first Earl was Sir John (XI.), who was known as *Iain
Glas*. He was born in 1635, and was created Earl of Caithness
in 1677. In 1661 he, by His Majesty's permission, took the
title of Earl of Breadalbane. John (XIV.) succeeded as lineal
descendant of Colin of Mocastle, second son of Robert (IX.),
and was created a Baron of the United Kingdom of Great
Britain in 1806 by the title of Baron Breadalbane of Taymouth,
county of Perth. John, the second Marquis and fifth Earl,
succeeded his father in 1834. He died without issue in 1862,
when the Marquisate of Breadalbane and the Earldom of
Ormelie in the Scottish Peerage became extinct. He was
succeeded in 1862 by the Scotch titles by Sir John Alexander
Gavin Campbell, sixth Earl of Breadalbane. He was succeeded
by his son, Gavin Campbell (XVII.), created Marquis of Breadalbane 1885. He died without issue, 1922, when the Marquisate and other U.K. honours became extinct.

The Scottish honours devolved upon his nephew, Iain
Edward Herbert Campbell, eighth Earl of Breadalbane, born
1885, died 1923, who was succeeded by a kinsman, Sir Charles
William Campbell, M.C., ninth Earl of Breadalbane and
Holland.

There is a Clan Campbell Society, with its headquarters in
Glasgow.

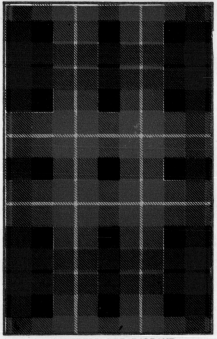

CAMPBELL, BREADALBANE.

THE CAMPBELLS OF CAWDOR.

Badge :—Roid (Wild Myrtle) or Garbhag an t-sléibhe
(Fir Club Moss).

JOHN, seventh Thane of Calder or Cawdor, married, in 1492, Isabel Rose, daughter of Kilravock, and, dying in 1494, left one posthumous child, a daughter, Muriel. Kilravock intended his heiress for his own grandson, her first cousin ; but Kilravock being pursued in a criminal process for robbery in joining Mackintosh for spoiling the lands of Urquhart of Cromarty, Argyll, the Justice-General, made the process easy to him, got the ward of Muriel's marriage of the King in 1495, and she was carried to Inveraray in the year 1499. In autumn of 1499 Campbell of Inverliver, with sixty men, came to receive the child on pretence of sending her south to school. As Inverliver came with little Muriel to Daltulich, in Strathnairn, he was close pursued by Alexander and Hugh Calder, her uncles, with a superior party. The conflict was sharp, and several were killed.

Muriel was married in 1510 to Sir John Campbell, third son of Argyll. He resided permanently at Cawdor from 1524 till 1546, the year of his death. Lady Muriel died in 1573, resigning her Thanedom in favour of her grandson, John (III.). Sir John, early in the seventeenth century, sold Croy, and disposed of Ferintosh to Lord Lovat, and mortgaged other lands in order to purchase, or rather to conquer, the island of Islay. The Cawdor family kept possession of Islay from 1612 to 1726, when it was purchased by Daniel Campbell of Shawfield.

Sir John Campbell, son of Sir Alexander (VII.), succeeded his father. He married Mary, eldest daughter and co-heiress of Lewis Pryce, and died in 1777. He was succeeded by his son, Pryce Campbell, M.P., who was succeeded by his son, John, who was elevated to the Peerage of Great Britain in 1796 by the title of Lord Cawdor of Castlemartin, Pembrokeshire. He died in 1821, and was succeeded by his son, John Frederick Campbell, Earl of Cawdor. He died 27th June 1860, and was succeeded by his eldest son, John Frederick Vaughan Campbell, second Earl of Cawdor. He died in 1898, and was succeeded by his son, Frederick Archibald Vaughan Campbell, third Earl of Cawdor, who was born in 1847. The fifth (and present) Earl, John Duncan Campbell, succeeded to the title in 1914.

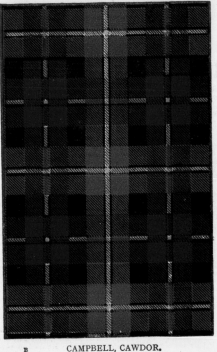

B   CAMPBELL, CAWDOR.

THE CAMPBELLS OF LOUDOUN.

War Cry :—" Cruachan " (A mountain near Loch Awe).
Badge :—Roid (Wild Myrtle) or Garbhag an t-sléibhe
(Fir Club Moss).

THE founder of the present House of Loudoun was Sir
Duncan Campbell, grandson of Hugh, third son of
Dougal Campbell, seventh Knight of Loch Awe. He
married Susanna, daughter and heiress of Sir Reginald Crawford of Loudoun, High Sheriff of Ayr, who died in 1303.
Robert I. in 1381 granted a charter converting Loudoun into
a free barony, with the lands of Stevenston. These lands were
possessed by the descendants of Sir Duncan and the heiress of
Loudoun from father to son to Hugh, the first Lord Loudoun,
then they again, with the title, went into the female line.
From Sir Duncan and his lady many highly respectable families
of the name of Campbell in Ayrshire are descended.

Sir Hugh Campbell of Loudoun was created Lord Campbell
of Loudoun in 1601. His son, John, Master of Loudoun, died
before him, leaving a daughter, Margaret, who succeeded to
all the honours of Loudoun in 1662, and married her name-
sake, Sir John Campbell of Lawers, who was created Earl
of Loudoun by Charles I. in 1633. His grandson, James Campbell, fell, a Major-General, at the battle of Fontenoy in 1745.

Hugh, third Earl of Loudoun, elder brother of the General,
died in 1731, and was succeeded by his son, John, fourth Earl,
who attained the highest military honours. He died, a General,
in 1782, and unmarried. The title thus reverted to his cousin,
Major-General James Mure Campbell, son of the General named
above who fell at Fontenoy, who married Flora, eldest daughter
of MacLeod of Raasay, by whom he had one child, Flora Mure
Campbell, who became Countess of Loudoun, and married, in
1804, General the Earl of Moira, Commander-in-Chief in Scotland, afterwards Governor-General of India, and who, in 1816,
was created Marquis of Hastings. The Countess Flora was
succeeded by her son, George, seventh Earl of Loudoun and
second Marquis of Hastings. On the death of Henry, ninth
Earl, the title went to his sister, Edith Maud, who married a
Mr. Clifton, with whom she assumed the name and Arms of
Abney-Hastings. The Countess died in 1874, and was succeeded by her son, Charles, eleventh Earl. He died in 1920,
and was succeeded in his Scottish titles by his niece, Edith
Maud Abney-Hastings, Countess of Loudoun.

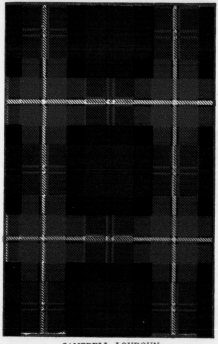

CAMPBELL, LOUDOUN.

THE CHISHOLMS.

Badge :—Raineach (Fern).

THE earliest traces of the Chisholms in Scotland are found to have been in the west of Roxburghshire. The clan is of Norman origin, and those of Berwick and Roxburgh came from Tindale, in England, and were successively called " De Chesé," " de Chesèholm," " de Cheseholme vel Chesholme." The original Border seat was the Barony of Chisholme, in Roxburghshire. In the fourteenth century Sir Robert de Chisholme came to the Highlands, and married the daughter and heiress of Sir Lauder of Quarrelwood and Constable of Urquhart Castle. He succeeded to the Lauder and other lands in the North. The Chisholms in the North becoming strong in wealth and followers, severed from the Border house and held independent sway. The North Country Chisholms, or, as they are called, the Strathglass Chisholms, six hundred years ago held lands in Forfar, Perth, Aberdeen, Moray, Inverness, Ross, Sutherland, and Caithness shires ; but now their whole estates are in Inverness and Ross shires, and even these are gone out of the line of chiefs. Erchless Castle is the seat, as it has been for centuries. Sir Robert and his descendants held their lands in the male line till 1884, when the then Chief, James Sutherland, and his son and heir took advantage of the Act of 1848 and barred the entail, in virtue of which alone they obtained possession. Had the entail not been so barred the property would have reverted to James Gordon Chisholm, grandson of Alexander (XXII.) the entailer. After the death, unmarried, in 1887, of Roderick (XXVIII.), the estates went by trust-disposition out of the entailer's family to the widow and daughters of James. At this time the male heir and Chief of the Chisholms entitled to the style of " The Chisholm " is Alexander, fourth son of John Chisholm, Comer, who settled in Australia over seventy years ago.

The Chief of the Chisholms is called in Gaelic " *An Siosalach*," and is the only Highland Chief who is entitled to the prefix " The."

CHISHOLM.

THE CLAN COLQUHOUN.

THE surname of this clan is a territorial one. The first who assumed it was Ingram, the successor of Humphry Kirkpatrick, who is designated in a charter of Luss by Malcolm, Earl of Lennox, to Malcolm, Laird of Luss, confirming John, Laird of Luss, his charter of the lands of Colchoun.

Sir Humphry Colquhoun, twelfth Laird of Luss, acquired the Heritable Coronership of Dumbartonshire in 1583. He died without issue, and was succeeded by his brother, Sir Alexander.

Sir Humphry, seventeenth Laird of Luss, married a daughter of Houston of that Ilk, by whom he had only a daughter, Anne, who in 1702 married James Grant of Pluscardine, second son of Grant of that Ilk; and being resolved that the young couple should succeed him in his whole estate and honours, in 1704 he resigned his baronetcy to the Crown, and obtained a new grant—to himself in life rent, to his daughter and son-in-law in fee, providing that their heirs should adopt the name and Arms of Colquhoun, and that the estates of Grant and Luss should never be conjoined. Sir Humphry died in 1715. James Grant succeeded as Sir James Colquhoun; but his elder brother dying without issue in 1719, he succeeded to the estates of Grant, and resuming that name, was succeeded in the Luss estates by his second son, Sir Ludovick, who, on the death of his elder brother, unmarried, also succeeded to the estates of Grant, and that of Luss went to his younger brother, James, who was created a Baronet in 1786 and, dying the same year, was succeeded by his son, Sir James, fifth Baronet of Colquhoun and Luss, who died in 1907, and was succeeded by his cousin, Sir Alan John Colquhoun. The present (seventh) Baronet is Sir Iain Colquhoun, D.S.O.

The principal seat of the Chief is Rossdhu House, Luss.

There is a Clan Colquhoun Society, with its headquarters in Glasgow.

COLQUHOUN.

CUMIN OR CUMMING.

Badge:—Lus Mhic Cuimin (Cumin plant).

SEVERAL clans of Norman origin like the Frasers and Cummings arrived in Scotland about the twelfth or thirteenth century. The Cummings belong to the Norman house "De Comines," a territorial name; the oldest form of the name in England is Comyn. The Comyns were closely allied to William the Conqueror. For 250 years, from 1080 to 1330, the Cumins flourished in strength in Badenoch.

Sir John, the Red Cumin or Comyn, was the first who was designed Lord of Badenoch. His son, John, called the Black Lord of Badenoch, was a somewhat unscrupulous competitor for the Crown of Scotland in the thirteenth century.

Edward, in pursuance of his nefarious schemes against Scotland, favoured the rival claims of John Baliol, which did not prevent the Lord of Badenoch from swearing fealty to the foe in 1292 (Rymer). Five years after he died a prisoner in England, leaving by his wife, daughter of John, and sister of King John Baliol, a son, who became Lord of Badenoch, called in turn the Red Cumin, an artful dissembler. A panderer to the King of England, he was on the point of betraying Robert Bruce to the latter, when he perished under the daggers of Bruce and Kirkpatrick in the church of Dumfries on the 10th of February 1306. He was the last Lord of Badenoch of the surname of Cumin.

The slaughter of the Red Cumin by Bruce inspired the whole clan with a desire to avenge his death. They opposed the King, who defeated them in 1308. The Earl was outlawed, and his forfeited estates were bestowed on the Keiths, Hays, and Douglases, whose good swords had helped to win the battle of Bannockburn. His only son married a daughter of the Earl of Pembroke, and died without heirs; but Jordanus Cumin, a kinsman of his, who got the lands of Inverallochy from Earl Alexander, became, it is said, ancestor of the Cumins of Culter, who, says Sir Robert Douglas, got a charter of these lands from James III. in 1477.

The old race is now represented by the Gordon-Cummings, Baronets of Gordonstoun, through the Cummings of Altyre, who succeeded to the name and Arms of Gordon by intermarriage.

The present (fourth) Baronet is Sir William Gordon Gordon-Cumming of Altyre and Gordonstoun, Co. Elgin.

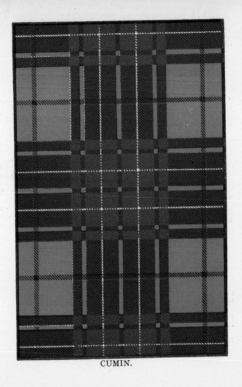

CUMIN.

THE DAVIDSONS.

Badge:—Lus nan cnàimhseag, or Braoileag (Red Whortleberry).

THIS clan associated themselves and took protection of and under William Mackintosh (VII.) of Mackintosh prior to 1350, and have ever since been regarded as a sept of Clan Chattan.

Kinrara, in his history (1676), says : " The Davidsons, styled of Invernahaven, in Badenoch, were, according to common tradition, originally a branch of the Comyns." After the downfall of the Comyns, Donald Du of Invernahaven associated himself with Clan Chattan, married a daughter of Angus (VI.) of Mackintosh, and became a leading member of Clan Chattan. The favour shown to him by the Captain of Clan Chattan roused the jealousy of another tribe, a jealousy which brought about the virtual extinction of the Davidsons.

The Davidsons, called *Clann Dà'idh* from their first known leader, David Du of Invernahaven, were chief actors in the two notable battles—Invernahaven (1370) and the North Inch of Perth (1396), and the losers in both battles.

The leading families are the Davidsons of Cantray, in Inverness, and the Davidsons of Tulloch, in Ross-shire.

About the year 1700 Alexander Davidson of Davidson, in Cromarty, married Miss Bayne of Tulloch, and purchased the estate from his father-in-law. The Baynes of Tulloch were for many generations of great position and influence in Ross-shire. Tulloch Castle is of ancient date, the keep having been built in 1166, and other parts of it in 1665. A branch of this family entered the service of France in the seventeenth century, having proved their descent to be noble for six generations prior to July 1629, as shown by the *Livre d'Or* in the imperial archives of France.

The Davidsons were almost annihilated at the battle of the North Inch, Perth, in 1396.

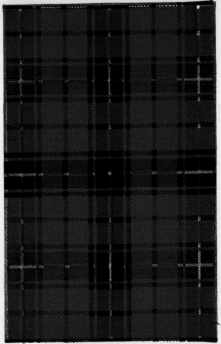

DAVIDSON.

THE DOUGLAS FAMILY.

War Cry :—"A Douglas ! A Douglas !"

THIS surname is a territorial one, from the wild pastoral
dale possessed by William de Douglas. A William de
Douglas witnessed a charter between 1174 and 1199.
His eldest son was Sir Archibald, who left two sons—Sir
William, and Andrew, ancestor of the Morton family. Sir
William died about 1274, and was succeeded by his son,
Sir William *le Hardi*. Sir William's son, "the Good" Sir
James, is known as the greatest captain of Bruce in the War
of Independence. He was killed, fighting against the Moors,
in Andalusia 1330. His son, William, fell at Halidon Hill,
and the next Lord of Douglas, Hugh, brother of Lord James,
made over the estates of the family in 1343 to his nephew,
Sir William.

The Douglases had, since the time of William the Hardy,
held the title of Lords of Douglas, but in 1357 Sir William
was made Earl of Douglas, and by marriage became Earl of
Mar. He died in 1384. His son, James, second Earl of
Douglas and Mar, fell at Otterburn in 1388, and, as he left
no legitimate issue, the direct male line of William the Hardy
and the Good Sir James now came to an end. His aunt had
married for her second husband one of her brother's esquires,
James of Sandilands, and through her Lord Torphichen, whose
barony was a creation of Queen Mary in 1564, became the heir-
general and representative at common law of the House of
Douglas. That House is now represented by such families as
those of Queensberry, Angus, Hamilton, Morton, etc.

There are also Douglases Baronets of Carr, and the Douglases
of Bonjedward, Timpindean, Baads, Delvine, etc.

DOUGLAS.

THE DRUMMONDS.

Badge :—Lus an Rìgh (Wild Thyme) or Cuileann (Holly).

THE exact origin of the Drummonds is difficult to determine, but the name is doubtless a territorial one, from the lands of Drummond or Drymen, in Stirlingshire.

There is every probability that at an early stage of their history the Drummonds had reached opulence and influence, as Malcolm Beg, so called from his low stature, sixth of the family, married Ada, daughter of Maldowen, Earl of Lennox, by Beatrix, daughter of Walter, the Lord High Steward.

Two of his grandsons became the prisoners of Edward I., and the eldest, Sir John, had, under compulsion, to swear fealty to the latter, and serve in his army against France; but his eldest son, Sir Malcolm Drummond, who married a daughter of Graham of Kincardine, was loyal to Bruce, and after Bannockburn received from him certain lands in Perthshire. His grandson, Sir John, married Mary Montifex, who brought him Cargill, Stobhall, and other places. He had a bitter feud with the Menteiths of Ruskie, in which his kinsman, Bryce Drummond, was slain, in 1330, and in pursuance of which he was accused of having slain three of the Menteiths, in compensation for which he was compelled to resign Rosneath. After this he retired to his lady's seat at Stobhall. Their daughter, Annabella, became Queen of Robert III.

James, fourth Lord Drummond, was created Earl of Perth in 1605. James, fourth Earl, was Lord Chancellor of Scotland, and followed the fortunes of James VII., who created him Duke of Perth. He died in 1716. James, his son, second Duke, was married to Lady Jane Gordon. He died in 1720, and was succeeded by his elder son, John, who was wounded at Culloden 1746.

James, second son of David, Lord Drummond, was created in 1610 Lord Maderty of Easter Craigton by James VI., but on the death of the third peer the title devolved on his nephew, Viscount Strathallan.

Among other families which may be mentioned are the Drummonds of Hawthornden, in Midlothian, cadets of the Perth Drummonds; the Drummonds of Concraig; the Drummonds of Stanmore, in Middlesex; and the Drummonds of Blair Drummond.

DRUMMOND

ERSKINE.

THE name is doubtless derived from the Barony of Erskine, in Renfrewshire, the proprietor of which was Henry de Erskine, in the reign of Alexander II. The family took a leading place in Scottish affairs at an early date. Mary, daughter of Sir William Erskine, was married to Sir Thomas Bruce, brother of King Robert I. Sir Robert Erskine, Chamberlain of Scotland 1350–57, married, first, Beatrix, daughter of Sir Alexander Lindsay of Crawford, by whom he had two sons—Thomas, his heir, and Malcolm, ancestor of the Erskines of Kinnoull. Sir Robert's eldest son, Thomas, married and had issue—Robert, created Lord Erskine, and John, ancestor of the Erskines of Dun.

The great-grandson of Robert, Lord Erskine—*i.e.*, Robert, fourth Lord—was killed at the battle of Flodden, and was succeeded by his son, James, as fifth Lord, who married and left two sons. The elder son, John, sixth Lord Erskine, was in 1565 created Earl of Mar, or was restored as seventeenth Earl of Mar by Queen Mary. He died in 1572, and was succeeded by his son, John, as eighteenth or second Earl. This nobleman was twice married, and his great-great-grandson (by his first marriage), John, twenty-second or sixth Earl, is well known in connection with the Scottish Rising of 1715. His descendant, John Francis Miller, twenty-fifth or ninth Earl, successfully claimed the Earldom of Kellie on the extinction of the junior branch of the family; but, dying without issue 1866, his cousin, Walter Coningsby, succeeded as twelfth Earl of Kellie, and also claimed the Earldom of Mar, but this claim was resisted by John Francis Erskine Goodeve, the nephew of the last (twenty-fifth or ninth) Earl. In 1875 the House of Lords decided that Walter Henry, thirteenth Earl of Kellie (son of the twelfth Earl), had made out his claim to the Earldom of Mar, dated 1565. He died in 1888, and his son, Walter John, is now twelfth Earl of Mar and fourteenth Earl of Kellie.

From the Erskines have also descended the Earls of Buchan and the Earls of Rosslyn.

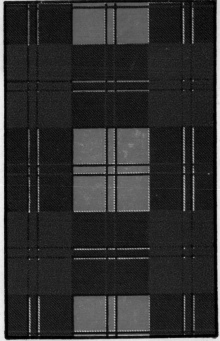

C   ERSKINE.

THE FARQUHARSONS.

War Cry :—" Càrn na cuimhne " (" Cairn of Remembrance ").
Badge :—Ròs-na-gréine (Little Sunflower) or Lus-nam-
ban-sith (Foxglove).

THE progenitor of the Farquharsons was Farquhar, fourth
son of Alexander Ciar, the third Shaw of Rothiemurchus.
Taking up their residence in Aberdeenshire, the descendants of this Farquhar were called Farquharsons. In their
early history the name of Farquhar's descendant, Finlay Mòr,
standard-bearer at Pinkie, where he fell, 1547, stands prominent, and from and after him the Farquharsons were termed
Clann Fhionnlaigh, or descendants of Finlay.

In the Rising of 1715 John Farquharson of Invercauld,
with four officers and 140 men, joined the Clan Chattan Regiment, in which he was Lieutenant-Colonel, and accompanying
it to England, was taken prisoner at Preston, where he remained for ten months.

At Culloden the Farquharsons mustered 300 men, and were
in the centre of the front line.

James Farquharson died in 1750, and was succeeded by his
son, also named James, who appears to have been, in 1745,
a Captain of Foot in the Hanoverian army. He died in 1806,
after having been in possession of the estates for fifty-six years.
He left no male issue, and was succeeded under the destination
of the entail by his only surviving child, Catherine, who
married Captain James Ross, R.N. (second son of Sir John
Lockhart-Ross, Bart., of Balnagowan), who took the name of
Farquharson, and died in 1810. He was succeeded by his son,
James Farquharson, who died in 1862, and was succeeded by
first his eldest, and later (1873) by his second son, Alexander
Haldane-Farquharson of Invercauld.

Among the other leading families of the name are the
Farquharsons of Monaltrie, Whitehouse, Haughton, Allargue
and Breda, and Finzean—all in Aberdeenshire.

On the extinction, in 1806, of the Invercauld family in the
male line, the chiefship of the Clan Farquharson became vested
in the family of Farquharson of Finzean.

The present Chief is Joseph Farquharson, R.A., of Finzean.

FARQUHARSON.

THE CLAN FERGUSON.

Badge :—Ròs-na-gréine (Little Sunflower) or Lus-nam-ban-slth (Foxglove).

ARGYLLSHIRE was probably the ancient home of this clan, and a branch, the *Clann Fhearghuis* of Stra-chur, long held lands at Strachur on Loch Fyne. They were also early established in Athole. The Chief was Baron Ferguson of Dunfallandy.

The Fergusons were among the gallant Athole men who followed the banner of Montrose in the Civil Wars, and in 1745 the Athole and Strathardle Fergusons were "out" with Prince Charlie.

The Fergusons are numerous in the parish of Balquhidder, where they have been for over six centuries. The name Ferguson has long been noted in Aberdeenshire. They are to be found there as landowners as early as the fourteenth century. Among the best known families are those of Kinmundy and Pitfour, many of whom distinguished themselves on the Bench and at the Bar. The clan also gained a footing in Banffshire and Kincardineshire, as well as in Fife and Forfar. The branch in Argyllshire was eclipsed in importance by being vassals at the Earls of Argyll, and yet they are to be found about Cowal and North Argyll.

In Ayrshire, and especially in Carrick, the clan have long held possessions. The ancient House of Kilkerran claim descent from Fergus, son of Fergus, who obtained a charter of lands in Ayrshire from Robert I.

In Dumfries and Galloway the name Ferguson is one of great antiquity. The Fergusons of Craigdarroch are among the old families in Scotland.

Sir Adam Ferguson, third Baronet, died in 1813, and was succeeded by his nephew, James, fourth Baronet, who died in 1838. He was succeeded by his son, Charles, fifth Baronet, who died in 1849, leaving the Right Honourable Sir James Ferguson, sixth Baronet, G.C.S.I., K.C.M.G., etc. He perished by the great earthquake in Jamaica in 1907. He was succeeded by his son, Sir Charles Ferguson of Kilkerran, as seventh Baronet.

FERGUSON.

THE CLAN FORBES.

War Cry :—" Lònach " (A mountain in Strath Don).
Badge :—Bealaidh (Broom).

THE clan took its name from the Aberdeenshire parish of Forbes. They are regarded as of common descent with the Mackays of Sutherlandshire, and are known as *Clann Mhorguinn* (Clan Morgan).

John of Forbes, the first on record, seems to have been a man of importance in the time of William the Lion. His name appears in a charter of Alexander, Earl of Buchan, dated 1236f His son, Alexander, lost his life when defending the castle oo Urquhart against Edward I. in 1303, but he left a son, als-Alexander, who fell at the battle of Dupplin in 1332. The post-humous son of the latter, Sir John Forbes of that Ilk, had four sons, and from the three younger sprang the Forbeses of Pit-sligo, Culloden, Waterton, and Foveran. He died in 1406.

Alexander, his eldest son, was raised to the Peerage by James I. as Baron Forbes. James, second Lord Forbes, had three sons—William, the third Lord ; Duncan, ancestor of the Forbeses of Corsindae and Monymusk ; and Patrick, ancestor of the Forbeses, Baronets of Craigievar, now Lord Sempill.

The Edinglassie Forbeses are a branch of the parent stock, and the Forbeses of Tolquhoun, a very old branch, acquired that estate in 1420, and were progenitors of the Lairds of Culloden.

Sir William Forbes, eighth Baronet of Craigievar, in 1884 succeeded his kinswoman as Lord Sempill, and was in turn succeeded in 1905 by his eldest son, Sir John Forbes Sempill.

According to information supplied by the late Dr. W. Forbes Skene to Mr. Elphinstone Dalrymple, it is ascertained that the present Forbes tartan was designed for the Pitsligo family in 1822. It was done by merely adding a white line to the Forty-Second. Prior to this date it is understood the Forbeses wore the Huntly tartan.

There is a traditionary connection between the clans of Forbes, Mackay, and Urquhart, originating from a famous hunter who is said to have slain a monstrous bear.

FORBES.

FORTY-SECOND ROYAL HIGHLAND REGIMENT
(THE BLACK WATCH).

THE origin of this gallant regiment dates as far back as 1729. The Highlands were then in an unsettled condition, and the Government entertained the idea of making use of the Highlanders as a means of protecting the country, and for this purpose six companies were formed. The men were all of respectable families, and were commanded by such well-known Highlanders as Lord Lovat, Campbell of Lochnell, Grant of Ballindalloch, Campbell of Finab, Campbell of Carrick, and Munro of Culcairn. Their duties consisted in carrying out the "Disarming Act" of 1716, and preventing depredations. In 1739 the Government determined to add to their number, which was raised from 525 to 1000. Up to this period each company was dressed in a tartan selected by its commander, but as the companies were now to be formed into one regiment it was necessary to have a uniform dress. The first Colonel, Lord Crawford, being a Lowlander, and having no tartan of his own, a new tartan, different from any other, was manufactured for the regiment. This ultimately became the well-known 42nd or Black Watch.

From the colour of the uniform of the Regular troops they were called *Saighdearan Dearg*—red soldiers, and the Highlanders from their sombre dress, *Freiceadan Dubh*, or Black Watch.

The Black Watch since its formation has taken a brilliant part in nearly every war its country has been engaged in, and has fought with honour in every quarter of the globe.

In 1887 a memorial cairn was erected to the Black Watch on the banks of the Tay near Aberfeldy. It bears inscriptions in Gaelic and English, stating that it was erected "in commemoration of the assembling together at Tay Bridge in 1739 of the six independent companies (afterwards increased to ten) of the *Freiceadan Dubh*, or Black Watch, who, after serving in several parts of the Highlands, were embodied into a regiment designated the 43rd, and afterwards the 42nd Royal Highlanders, whose first muster took place in May 1740 near Tay Bridge."

FORTY-SECOND (BLACK WATCH).

THE CLAN FRASER.

War Cry :—" A' Mhór-fhaiche " (" The Great Field ") and later,
" Caisteal Dhùni " (" Castle Downie ").
Badge :—Iubhar (Yew).

THOUGH of Norman origin, the Frasers have attained to
the position of a true Highland clan. The name is spelt
variously as Frazer, Freser, Frezel, etc., and is referred to
the old French *freze*—strawberry. Seven strawberry leaves
form part of the armorial bearings of the Frasers. We find a
Gilbert of Fraser is witness of a charter to the Monastery of
Coldstream, in the reign of Alexander I., anno 1109. Sir Simon
Fraser of Oliver Castle was put to death in London by Edward
I., but his brother, Alexander, carried on the line of the family,
and seems to have been the first Fraser who possessed estates
in the Highlands. His grandson fell at Halidon Hill in 1333,
leaving a son, Hugh, first designed of Lovat, and progenitor of
the Frasers of Knock and Foyers. Hugh, sixth of this family
and second of Lovat, was made a Baron by James I. about 1460.

Simon, eleventh Lord Lovat, was deeply involved in the
Jacobite rising of 1745. His title was attainted. It was revived
as a British Peerage in 1837, when Thomas Fraser of Strichen
and Lovat was created Lord Lovat, and became twenty-first
Chief in succession from Simon Fraser.

Lord Lovat died in 1875, and was succeeded by his son,
Simon, who died in 1887, leaving his second son, Sir Simon
Joseph Fraser, K.T., as the present Lord Lovat.

The Frasers, Baronets of Ledclune, descend from Hugh,
first Lord Lovat, through Alexander, his second son.

The Frasers of Saltoun are descended from William, second
son of Sir Alexander Fraser of that Ilk. Sir Alexander, ninth
of this family, on the death of his cousin, Lord Saltoun, without issue in 1669, was served heir-of-line to George, Lord
Abernethy of Saltoun, his grandfather, and his descendant,
Alexander, is now eighteenth Lord Saltoun.

FRASER.

THE CLAN GORDON.

War Cry :—" A Gordon ! A Gordon !"
Badge :—Iadh-shlat, Eitheann (Ivy).

THIS surname is territorial. The first Gordon of whom we
have any distinct trace is Richard, who was Lord of the
Barony of Gordon in Berwickshire, who in 1150 and 1160
granted from that estate a piece of land to the monks of St.
Mary at Kelso.

In the time of King Robert the Bruce, Sir Adam, Lord of
Gordon, obtained a grant of the Lordship of Strathbogie in
Aberdeenshire. His great-grandson, Sir Adam, was slain in
battle, 1402, leaving an only child, Elizabeth, who married
Alexander, second son of Seton of Seton. Her only son, Alex-
ander, was created Earl of Huntly.

George, second Earl, left four sons. The second, Adam
married Elizabeth, Countess of Sutherland.

In 1599 the sixth Earl of Huntly was created Marquis. The
fourth Marquis received in 1684 the title of Duke of Gordon
from Charles II. On the death of George, fifth Duke, in 1836,
the title became extinct, but the Marquisate of Huntly went to
the Earl of Aboyne, lineally descended from George, fourth
son of George, second Marquis of Huntly.

The Earls of Aberdeen, so created in 1682, are descended
from Patrick Gordon of Methlic (cousin of the Earl of Huntly),
who fell at the battle of Arbroath in 1445. They were afterwards designed as the Lairds of Methlic and Haddo.

Two regiments named the " Gordon Highlanders " have been
raised from this clan. The first was the old 81st, formed in 1777
and disbanded 1783. The second was the 92nd or Gordon Highlanders, raised in 1794.

On the raising of the Gordon Highlanders a yellow strip was
introduced into the Black Watch pattern for their regimental
use, and since then the Gordons have discontinued the use of
the Huntly tartan except on full-dress occasions.

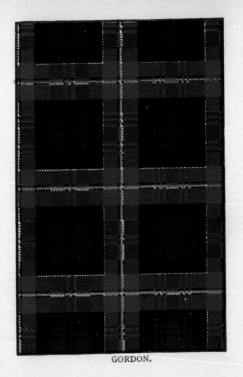

GORDON.

THE CLAN GRAHAM.

Badge :—Buaidh-chraobh, na Labhras (Laurel).

THE first authentic appearance of this surname seems to be about 1143-47, when William of Graham is one of the witnesses of David I., Holyrood Charter. He afterwards obtained the lands of Abercorn and Dalkeith. His grandson and representative, David Graham, obtained from William the Lion, before 1214, certain lands near Montrose. David's son acquired, under the succeeding monarch, by exchange of land belonging to him in Galloway, from Patrick, Earl of Dunbar, the lands of Dundaff and Strathearn ; and from the Earl of Lennox those of Strathblane and Mugdock. His son, Sir David of Dundaff, married a daughter of the Earl of Strathearn, by whom he had three sons—Sir Patrick, Sir John, and Sir David. Sir John was termed "the right hand" of the patriot Wallace, and fell at the battle of Falkirk 1298.

Sir William, *Dominus de Graham et Kincardine*, obtained from Robert, Duke of Albany, a charter containing an entail of Old Montrose. Patrick, his grandson, was created Lord Graham by James II. about 1445. The third Lord was created Earl of Montrose by James IV. in 1504. He fell at Flodden 1513.

The Grahams of the Borders are descended from Sir John Graham of Kilbride, second son of Malise, Earl of Strathearn, and afterwards of Menteith. Sir John was ancestor of the Grahams of Gartmore, in Perthshire.

To the Marquis of Graham (afterwards Duke of Montrose) Highlanders are indebted for carrying through Parliament in 1782 an Act repealing the disgraceful Act of 1747, which made penal the use of the Highland garb.

The Chief of the clan is the Duke of Montrose (James Graham, C.B., C.V.O., V.D.).

GRAHAM.

THE CLAN GRANT.

War Cry :—" Stand fast, Craigellachie."
Badge :—Giuthas (Pine Tree).

HISTORICALLY speaking, the Grant Chiefs are undoubtedly Norman. The name, too, despite Gaelic possi-
bilities, is Norman; it is simply a modification of the
French *grand*, English " grand." The first Grants mentioned
in Scottish records are Lawrence and Robert le Grant in 1258.
Sir Lawrence was Sheriff of Inverness, and Robert held lands
in Nairnshire. The name was common in England in Norman
times, especially in Lincoln and Notts; and there was a famous
Normandy family of Grante whose motto, also, was " Stand
fast " (*Tenons Ferme*). The first Grant lands are Stratherrick,
where they are found in the fourteenth century.

John Grant of Freuchie and Grant married, in 1484, a
daughter of Ogilvie of Deskford, and left three sons—James,
his successor, ancestor of the Earls of Seafield; John, on whom
he bestowed the Barony of Corrimony in 1509; and John Mór
(a natural son), to whom he gave Glenmoriston.

Sir James Grant of that Ilk and his son, Ludovic, eighth
Laird of Freuchie, adhered to William II. of Scotland (or
Orange), and were with the clan in the fight at the Haughs
of Cromdale. In 1715 and 1745 he adhered to the House of
Hanover, but Glenmoriston was " out " for the Stewarts. The
marriage of Ludovic to Margaret, daughter of James, Earl of
Seafield, brought that title into the family in the person of
her grandson, Sir Lewis Alexander Grant.

There are three Baronets of the surname—Dalvey, 1688;
Monymusk, 1705; and Ballindalloch (a Macpherson), 1838.

The eleventh Earl of Seafield died of wounds received in
action, 12th November 1915, and was succeeded in his Scottish
Peerages by his daughter, Nina Caroline Ogilvie Grant, as
Countess of Seafield, while the late Earl's brother fell heir
both to the Barony of Strathspey and to the chiefship of
Clan Grant.

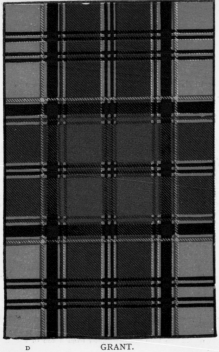

D   GRANT.

THE CLAN GUNN.

Badge :—Aitionn (Juniper) or Lus nan laoch (Roseroot).

THIS clan is of Norse origin. The Gunns were a warlike clan of Caithness and Sutherland ; the name is derived from the Norse word *gunnr*—war.

The Gunns and the Keiths were for ever at enmity. Lachlan Gunn of Braemor had an only daughter, Helen, who was famous for her beauty, and the day of her marriage with her cousin Alexander was fixed ; but Dugald Keith, a retainer of Keith of Ackergill, whose advances she had repelled, surrounded her father's house with a body of armed Keiths, slew many of the Gunns, who were unprepared for an attack, and carried off the girl to Ackergill, where she became the victim of her abductor, and eventually threw herself from the summit of the tower.

Raid upon raid ensued now, and during one of these, in 1426, a desperate battle was fought between the two clans at Harpsdale, eight miles from Thurso. The conflict was rancorous and bloody, but indecisive.

About the middle of the fifteenth century the Chief of the clan was George, who lived with barbaric pomp in his castle at Clyth. From the office he held he was known as Crouner Gunn, but by the natives as " *Am Bràisteach Mór,*" from a large silver brooch which fastened his plaid. Weary of the feud, he and the Chief of the Keiths agreed to meet with twelve horsemen a-side at the Chapel of St. Tears and settle it amicably. This was in 1464. The Keiths came with twenty-four men—two on each horse—and attacked the Gunns ; the latter fought desperately, and were cut to pieces. George Gunn was slain and stripped of his arms, armour and brooch. Soon after William MacKames, a kinsman of the Gunns, killed George of Ackergill and his son, with ten men, at Drummay.

The patronymic of Gunn of Kilearnan is *Mac-Sheumais-Chataich.*

The chiefship is considered to belong to the family of Gunn of Rhives, who are descended from a son of the fifth Chief.

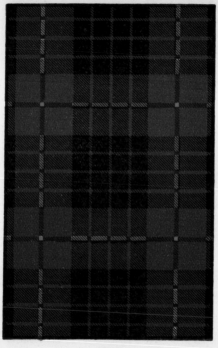

GUNN.

THE HENDERSONS
(MacKendricks).

Badge :—Canach (Cotton Grass).

T HE Hendersons claim descent from *Eanruig Mór Mac Righ
Neachtan*—Bigh Henry, son of King Nectan. It is difficult to determine when the descendants of *Eanruig Mór*
became possessed of that tract of country embracing Glencoe,
both sides of Loch Leven, and Ardnamurchan. According to
tradition, the Chiefs of the clan held their seats at Callart, on
the north side of Loch Leven, and as late as the fifteenth century a chieftain of the clan held the lands of Callart. The
Glencoe Hendersons clung to their lands under the vassalage
of the Lords of the Isles, and were known generally as the
MacIains of Glencoe, a name applied to them through their
first Chief of the Clan MacDonald, "*Iain Fraoch*," who flourished
in 1346. He was brother of John, first Lord of the Isles, and
natural son of Angus Og of Islay. Gregory says : " Angus Og
had a natural son, known as *Iain Fraoch*, or Heather John, on
whom his brother, John, Lord of the Isles, bestowed Glencoe."
Iain Fraoch's mother is said to have been a daughter of one
Dugald MacHendry—*i.e.*, Dugald Henderson—chief or head-
man of Glencoe. They lived at Inverlochy for a time, where
their first son and heir was born, who in due time became the
first MacIain of Glencoe, or, as the Glencoe people called him,
Iain Abrach (John of Lochaber). *Iain Fraoch*, although a
MacDonald, appointed Hendersons as his bodyguard, and until
the death of the last MacIain Chief they were accorded the
honour of the first "lift" of the remains when borne forth for
burial.

The Hendersons of Caithness have no connection with those
of Glencoe. They are descendants of Hendry, son of George
Gunn, Crouner of that county. There are also Hendersons
in Fordell, Fifeshire, who claim as a cadet of their family
Alexander Henderson, the great divine and leader of the
Reformation.

HENDERSON.

THE JACOBITE TARTAN

JACOBITES is the name applied after the Rising of 1688 to the adherents of the Stewarts, more particularly to those who rose in 1715 and 1745 or openly sympathised with them then or later.

The northern portion of Scotland was much in sympathy with the House of Stewart, and in 1745 the majority of the Highland clans rose with Bonnie Prince Charlie, and their Chiefs suffered with them after the defeat at Culloden. It is not therefore to be wondered that a Jacobite tartan was manufactured, and was largely worn by many ladies and gentlemen of rank who sympathised with the Stewarts. This tartan, the pattern or set of which is given here, "was worn," says Mr. Smith, "as one of the emblems of the Jacobites. We had it from a lady of rank who has still in her possession a silk scarf (or plaid) of it which was manufactured in 1712 for a lady who was a most zealous Jacobite."

Many secret signs and emblems were adopted by the Jacobites prior to the Rising of 1715, and this Jacobite tartan was one of them. Doubtless it was adopted and worn as a symbol to others of secret political opinions, like the S (for Stewart) in the open-work of the claymore-hilt or the legend " No Union " on its blade. Another badge of Jacobitism was " The White Cockade," so often referred to in Jacobite literature.

> " My love was born in Aberdeen,
>   The bonniest lad that e'er was seen,
>   But now he mak's my heart full sad ;
>   He's ta'en the field wi' his white cockade.
>
>   O ! he's a rantin' rovin' blade,
>   O ! he's a brisk and bonnie lad,
>   Betide what may, my heart is glad
>   To see my lad wi' his white cockade.
>
> I'll sell my sock, I'll sell my reel,
>   My rippting-kaim and spinning-wheel,
>   To buy my lad a tartan plaid,
>   A braid-sword, dirk, and a white cockade.
>   O ! he's a rantin' rovin' blade, etc."

JACOBITE.

JOHNSTON.

Badge :—Red Hawthorn.

THIS is one of the Border clans, whose origin goes back to the thirteenth century in the person of Sir Gilbert de Johnstoun, son of John, who lived about 1200. He had a son, Gilbert, who was father of Sir John, living 1296. Sir John was father of John and Gilbert de Johnstoun ; the latter was succeeded by his son, Sir John. The last named had one son, Adam, who was ancestor of the Johnstons of Newbie, Mylnefield, and Galabank. The above-named Adam Johnston was twice married, and had by his first wife a son, John, ancestor of the Johnstons of Westerhall, and by his second wife he had Sir Gilbert, ancestor of the Johnstons of Elphinstone. Sir James of Westerhall was created Lord Johnstone 1633 and Earl of Hartfell 1643. The Earl was succeeded by his son, James, created Earl of Annandale and Hartfell 1661. The second Earl was succeeded by his son, William, who was created Marquess of Annandale 1701. He was twice married. By his first marriage he had James, second Marquess, who died without issue 1730, and Henrietta, who married Charles, first Earl of Hopetoun ; she is now represented by the Hope-Johnstones of Annandale, the first Marquess, who died 1792. From Matthew, first of Westerhall, descended Sir James, who died 1699. He left two sons, Sir John, who died without issue, and his brother, Sir William, who left two sons, Sir James, third Baronet of Westerhall, and John, whose son, Richard, was created a Baronet in 1795, whose grandson, Harcourt, third Baronet, was created Baron Derwent 1881. The third Baronet of Westerhall left six sons. John, fifth son, was the ancestor of the Johnstones of Alva. The North Country Johnstones descend from Stephen Cherrie, who married Margaret, daughter and heiress of Sir Andrew Garioch, with whom he obtained a Barony of Johnston, who gave the name to his descendants. He is now represented by Sir Thomas Alexander Johnston (eleventh Baronet) of that Ilk, Hilton and Caskieben.

JOHNSTON.

THE CLAN LAMONT.

Badge :—Craobh-ubhal fhiadhain (Crab-apple tree) or
Machall-monaidh (Dryas).

THE surname Lamont or Lamond is from the Norse *laga-madr*—a lawman.
The first of the clan of whom there is absolute historical evidence is Ferchar, who flourished about 1200. Ferchar's grandson, Laumun, was the first to use the name which has since become hereditary. About 1238 Duncan, son of Ferchar, and this Laumun, son of Malcolm, son of Ferchar, granted certain lands at Kilmun, etc., to the monks of Paisley.

About 1646 the Lamont country was ravaged by the Campbells, who carried about two hundred prisoners to Dunoon and massacred them at the Gallowhill. A memorial to commemorate the event was erected by the Clan Lamont Society in 1906.

From the thirteenth to the seventeenth century the chiefs used the barony title of "Inveryne," with Toward Castle for part of that time as principal residence. In 1646 Ardlamont became the seat of the Chief.

The Lamonts of Knockdow claim descent from Geoffrey (or Gorre), son of John Lamont, alive in 1431.

The families of Auchagoyll (now Otter) and Auchinshellich (or Willowfield) both descended from Walter, son of Sir John Lamont of Inveryne ; Cowston from Patrick Lamont, Crowner of Cowal in 1450. Silvercrags was of Robert, third lawful son of Sir John (X.). Stilaig was held by Archibald, second son of Sir John, and his successors till about 1643, when Sir James (XIV.) granted it to his brother Archibald.

The present Chief is Major John Henry Lamont, late 9th Lancers, who was born in 1854.

There is a Clan Lamont Society, founded in 1895. Its headquarters are in Glasgow.

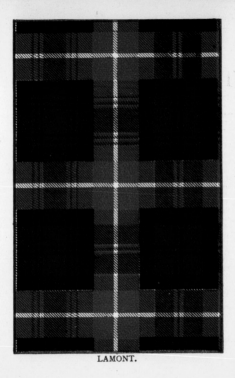

LAMONT.

THE LESLIES.

THIS surname is derived from the lands of Leslie, in Fife. The first of the name on record was Bartholf of Leslie in the reign of William the Lion.

David, eighth of Leslie, was one of the hostages for the ransom of James I. in 1424. George, tenth of Leslie, was the first Earl of Rothes, and was so created by James II. William, third Earl, fell with his Royal master at Flodden. George, fourth Earl, accompanied James V. to France. His son, Norman, Master of Rothes, after being engaged in the murder of Cardinal Beaton, was slain in battle in Picardy in 1554. The Earl died at Dieppe in 1558. John, seventh Earl of Rothes, carried the Sword of State at the Coronation of Charles II. in Scone Palace, 1651. In 1680 he was created Duke of Rothes, but died the following year, leaving a daughter, the Countess, whose eldest son, John, succeeded by entail to the Earl of Rothes, while Thomas, her second son, carried on the honours of Haddington.

Sir Alexander Leslie (first Earl of Leven in 1641) was a famous warrior. His title is now united with that of Melville.

Sir Patrick Leslie of Pitcairlie, second son of the fifth Earl of Rothes, was created Lord Lindores by James VI. in 1600. His title has been dormant since 1775.

A famous branch were the Leslies of Balquhain, in Aberdeenshire. Sir George, the founder of it, got a grant of that estate from David II. by charter, dated 1340. Four Count Leslies sprang from this family alone. Sir Andrew Leslie, third of Balquhain, had a bitter feud with the Forbeses. He was slain 1420. Sir William, seventh of Balquhain, rebuilt the old castle of that name, which burned down by the Forbeses, and died in 1545. The castle is now in ruins.

The present male representative of the Leslie Clan is Sir Norman Roderick Alexander David Leslie, eighth Baronet, C.B.E., of Wardis.

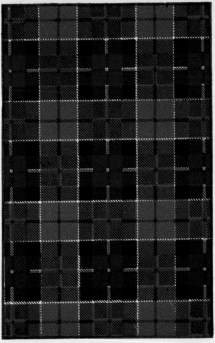

LESLIE.

THE LINDSAYS.

Badges :—Rue, and Lime Tree.

THE name Lindsay is an old English one, denoting "Lime Tree Isle," of which there were two—one in Lincoln and one in Essex. From the place-name came the surname Lindsay, originally De Lindsay. The family came early to Scotland, and were there established in David I.'s time.

Sir David Lindsay of Crawford was living about 1340. He had two sons : (1) Alexander of Glenesk, father of David, created Earl of Crawford 1398 ; and (2) Sir William of the Byres. The grandson of the first Earl—David, third Earl—left two sons—Alexander, fourth Earl, and Walter of Edzell. On the death of the sixteenth Earl, the title went to the Lindsays of the Byres, passing over the Edzell family.

David, ninth Earl of Crawford, left two sons : (1) Sir David of Edzell, whose line failed in 1744 ; and (2) John of Balcarres, father of David, created Lord Lindsay of Balcarres 1633, whose son, Alexander, was created Earl of Balcarres 1651. This Earl's grandson, James, fifth Earl of Balcarres, left two sons : (1) Alexander, sixth Earl, who was twenty-third Earl of Crawford, 1808, on the failure of the direct line of Lindsay of Byres. The present (twenty-seventh) Earl of Crawford and Balcarres is David Alexander Edward Lindsay, K.T., P.C.

The Lindsays, known as "The Light Lindsays," are about the only Lowland clan who have formed themselves into a Society. This they did in October 1897, under the presidency of the Right Hon. The Earl of Crawford, K.T., Chief of the clan.

To the Clan Lindsay we are indebted for that exquisite song, "Auld Robin Gray," which is the composition of Lady Anne Lindsay, eldest daughter of James Lindsay, fifth Earl of Balcarres. She was born 1750.

The headquarters of the Clan Society are in Edinburgh, with a branch in Glasgow.

LINDSAY.

THE LOGANS OR MACLENNANS.

War Cry :—" Druim nan deur " (" The Ridge of Tears ").
Badge :—Conasg (Furze).

THE traditional account of the origin of the Maclennans is as follows : In a feud between the Frasers and the Lobans (or Logans), the latter were defeated at the battle of Drumderfit, near Kessock Ferry, and their leader, a brave warrior called Gilligorm, slain. Gilligorm left a posthumous son, born among the Frasers, by whom his back was broken to prevent him from growing up strong and warlike enough to avenge the death of his father. This son was called Crotair MacGilligorm (the humph-back son of Gilligorm). He was educated at Beauly Priory, took Holy Orders, and eventually moved to the West Coast, where he founded and built two churches—one at Kilmuir in Skye, and the other in Glenelg. This was about the beginning of the thirteenth century. Crotair married, as priests in the Highlands frequently did in those days, and had, with other issue, a son, whom he called *Gille Fhinnein*, in honour of St. Finnan, and whose descendants became known as the Maclennans.

The Maclennans were at one time numerous in Kintail, in Ross-shire, and tradition has preserved the name of a renowned warrior, Donald Maclennan, who took a prominent part in the great feud between Kintail and Glengarry about 1600. The Maclennans appear to have been, on some occasions, the standard-bearers of Kintail, and at the battle of Auldearn, in 1645, a certain Roderick Maclennan and his brother, Donald, were killed while bravely defending the banner of their Chief.

Loban, or Lobban, is a Morayshire name. William Lobane appears in 1564 as tenant in Drumderfit, in the Black Isle, where the family were so long tenants that the local proverb says, " As old as the Lobans of Drumderfit." " It seems," says Dr. Alexander MacBain, " to be from the Gaelic *lòban*, a kind of basket peat-cart or sledge, under which the ' first original ' of them hid—a Maclennan he was—in terror, and escaped with the nickname as the only detriment."

E   LOGAN or MACLENNAN.

THE CLAN MACALISTER.

Badge :—Fraoch gorm (Common Heath).

IT is generally understood that this clan branched off from the main Clan Donald stem early in the thirteenth century. They are supposed to be descended from Alister Mor, son of Donald de Ile, and younger brother of Angus Mor.

In 1366 Ranald, son of Alexander, appears on the scene as heir to Clan Alister. Ranald had his residence in Kintyre, where the Clan Alister at a later time are found largely to abound. In 1481 Charles MacAlister was appointed by James III. to the Stewartry of Kintyre, and at the same time received a charter for a considerable grant of lands in that peninsula. Charles was succeeded by his son, John, who is styled " John of the Lowb," now rendered Loup, from the Gaelic *lub*, a curve or bend, this being the configuration of the shore which bounded the ancient patrimony of the Clan Alister.

During the fifteenth and sixteenth centuries members of the clan obtained settlements in Bute and Arran, and their descendants are there to this day.

In the latter half of the sixteenth century a new branch of Clan Alister of Kintyre sprung into existence—namely, the family of Tarbert. The heads of the House became hereditary Constables of Tarbert Castle. To this branch belongs Principal MacAlister of Glasgow University.

Gory MacAlester of Loup had a son, Alexander, who succeeded him. He fought at Killiecrankie, under Viscount Dundee, and afterwards served with the Royal army in Ireland against William of Orange. His son died without issue, so he was succeeded by his brother, Charles, who married a daughter of Lamont of that Ilk. His son, Charles, born in 1765, married the heiress of Kennox, in Ayrshire, and added the Arms of Somerville to his own.

The present Chief of the clan is Lieut.-Col. Charles Godfrey Somerville MacAlester, who succeeded in 1903.

MACALISTER.

THE MACALPINES.

War Cry :—" Cuimhnich bàs Ailpein " (" Remember the death of Alpin ").
Badge :—Giuthas (Pine Tree).

WHILE the personal name Alpin or Alpine is from the Welsh, it came into the Gaelic from Strathclyde and from the Picts as well. " The general appellation of *Sìol Ailpein*," says Skene in his *Highlanders of Scotland*, " has been usually given to a number of clans situated at considerable distance from each other, but who have hitherto been supposed to possess a common descent, and that from Kenneth MacAlpine, the ancestor of a long line of Scottish kings. These clans are the Clan Gregor, the Grants, the Mackinnons, Macquarries, Macnabs, and MacAulays, and they have at all times claimed the distinction of being the noblest and most ancient of the Highland clans. ' *Is rioghail mo dhream* ' (' My race is Royal ') was the proud motto of the MacGregors, and although the other clans have for centuries acquiesced in the justice of that motto, yet this lofty boast must fall before a rigid examination into its truth; for the authority of the Manuscript of 1450 puts it beyond all doubt that that origin was altogether unknown at that period, and that these clans in reality formed part of the tribe of Ross." The principal tribe was always admitted to be that of Clan Gregor.

That the MacAlpines are of ancient origin is maintained by the Gaelic saying, " *Cnuic is uillt is Ailpeinich* " (" Hills and streams and MacAlpines "), the inference being that the origin of the MacAlpines was contemporary with the formation of hillocks and streams.

The ancient crest of the MacAlpines is A boar's head couped gules, goutty sanguine : with the Gaelic motto, " *Cuimhnich bàs Ailpein* " (" Remember the death of Alpin "), alluding to the murder of King Alpin.

The seat of the Chief of the clan is said to have been at Dunstaffnage, Argyllshire.

MACALPINE.

THE MACARTHURS.

War Cry :—" Eisd ! O Eisd ! " (" Listen ! O Listen ! ").
Badge :—Roid (Wild Myrtle) or Garbhag an t-sléibhe
(Fir Club Moss).

THE MacArthurs are a branch of the great Clan Campbell, and trace their descent from the original stock ; they indeed, for a long time, disputed the seniority with the House of Argyll. In the thirteenth century the Campbells presented two great divisions—those of *MacCailein Mór* and *MacArtair*, and the latter maintained their right to the chief-ship, and were, in fact, at the head of the clan, a position which they retained till the time of James I.—the beginning of the fifteenth century. In 1374 the lands of Strachur were resigned by Ewan Campbell, and granted by Robert II. to Arthur Campbell, his son. This Arthur Campbell is probably the person from whom the MacArthurs of Upper Cowal derived their patronymic, as they were in possession of this district long before the Campbells of Argyll got possession of Inveraray.

The MacArthurs having espoused the cause of Bruce, were rewarded by ample gifts of the forfeited estates of the Mac-Dougalls of Lorn. The Chief was also appointed Captain of the Castle of Dunstaffnage, and the clan was in possession of extensive territory in the county of Argyll.

John MacArthur was beheaded by the command of James I., and his lands were forfeited. Since then the *MacCailein Mór* branch have held the chiefship, and gradually acquired much property in the county.

A family of MacArthurs were for many generations hereditary pipers to the MacDonalds of Sleat. The most celebrated of the family was Charles, whose musical education was perfected by Patrick Og MacCrimmon.

It is maintained that the chiefship of the clan rests in the family of the MacArthurs of Proaig, Islay, some of whose ancestors were armourers to the MacDonalds of Islay.

MACARTHUR.

THE CLAN MACAULAY.

Badge :—Muileag (Cranberry) or Giuthas (Pine Tree).

THERE were two Clans MacAulay. The best known were the MacAulays of Ardincaple, in Dumbartonshire, a property disposed of by the twelfth Chief in the eighteenth century to the Campbells of Argyll. They have no connection with the Lewis Clan MacAulay. The MacAulays of Ardincaple are believed to be of the family of Lennox, for in a charter granted by Maldowen, Earl of Lennox, to Sir Patrick Grahame, is Aulay, the Earl's brother, as also in another charter by the same Earl to William, son of Arthur Galbraith, the witnesses are Duncan and Aulay, the Earl's brothers.

Sir Aulay MacAulay of Ardincaple appears in 1587 in the Roll of the Landlords and Bailies in the Highlands and Isles as one of the principal vassals of the Earl of Lennox.

The last portion of the clan territory passed out of the hands of the twelfth Chief in 1767, when Ardincaple was sold to the Duke of Argyll.

The first MacAulay of Lewis on record is Donald *Cam*, mentioned in 1610, who is said to have been captured along with Torquil Dubh in 1597, but escaped. Donald Cam's son, Angus of Brenish, was killed at Auldearn Battle, 1645. His son, Dugald, succeeded him as *Fear Bhrenis*, and his son was Rev. Aulay Macaulay, minister of Harris, married to Rev. Kenneth Morrison's daughter, of Stornoway. His son was the Rev. John Macaulay of Cardross, whose son, Zachery, was father of the famous Lord Macaulay.

The Lewis MacAulays had namesakes, no doubt kinsmen, on the mainland, vassals to the MacKenzies. Lochbroom is said to have been their original possession, a district which the heiress of Duncan MacAulay is said to have given with her hand to the Chief of the MacKenzies in the fourteenth century. The MacAulays of the mainland are coupled with the Macleays and MacIvors in the fifteenth century as giving trouble to the Earl of Ross and his tenants.

MACAULAY.

THE MACBEANS.

Badge :—Bocsa, or Craobh aighban (Boxwood) or Lus nan
cnàimhseag, or Braoileag (Red Whortleberry).

THIS clan formed a branch of the Clan Chattan under
Mackintosh. The Gaelic form of the word is *Mac-
Bheathain*. The original habitat of the MacBeans appears to have been the valley of the Nairn and Strathdearn,
and latterly Upper Strathspey and Badenoch.

The clan history is merged in that of the rest of Clan
Chattan. The chief family was that of Kinchyle, in Dores,
a representative of whom signs the Clan Chattan Bond of 1609.
Angus, who signs this Bond, obtained a feu of Kinchyle in
1610.

The other leading families of MacBean were those of Faillie
and of Drummond, with the existent family of Tomatin, descended from the Faillie family. The first of the Tomatin
family was Bean, son of Donald MacGilliphatrick, first of
Faillie. Bean got a charter from the Earl of Moray in 1639
of the lands of Tomatin. His sons, Evan and William, succeeded him in turn. William's son was John, whose son
was Lewis. He established a business of Kinchyle, in Glasgow, to enable
him to save his Highland property. His sons, William and
Duncan, succeeded him in turn. The present representative
of the family is Lachlan MacBean, Esq. of Tomatin, Inverness-
shire.

The surname MacBean or MacBain is found in Perthshire
and parts of Argyllshire as MacVean. Indeed, the Perthshire,
or, rather, Athole, Macbeths are known in Gaelic as *Mac-
Bheathain*, as also in that county is the name of King Macbeth.

MACBEAN.

MACBETH.

THIS name appears often in Scottish records of the eleventh, twelfth, and thirteenth centuries.

Macbeth (or MacBethad MacFinlaeg, as he was called in contemporary chronicles) was a king of Scotland. He ascended the throne in 1040 and reigned seventeen years. He inherited the rule of the province of Moray from Finlaeg, his father; and his wife was Gruoch, daughter of Boete, son of Kenneth III., a fact which possibly gave him a claim on the Scottish throne. He defeated and slew King Duncan, his predecessor. He was slain at Lumphanan, in Aberdeenshire, on the 5th of December 1056. His body was interred in Iona, the common sepulchre for many centuries of the Scottish kings. His followers were able to place his nephew, Lulach, on the throne.

Two learned families practised medicine in the Hebridean Isles in the sixteenth and seventeenth centuries, their names were Macbeth and Beaton or Bethune; and these two names were in the seventeenth and eighteenth centuries merged in English into the one surname of Beaton. The similarity of name and profession easily led to this. The Macbeths practised in Islay and Mull; the Beatons were located in Skye. The Macbeths were the learned *ollamhs* or doctors of Islay, famed not only for medicine but for lore. They were hereditary physicians to the MacDonalds of the Isles. The Mull Macbeths were physicians to Maclean of Duart; another of them was Fergus M'Veagh in Pennycross, Mull, possessor of a Medical MS., now in Edinburgh University which gives a valuable genealogy of the family. The other Beaton family were the medical authorities for Skye in the seventeenth century; they are claimed as real Beatons, or Bethunes, from Fifeshire.

MACBETH.

THE MACCALLUMS.

THE district of Lorn, Argyllshire, is generally regarded as the habitat of the MacCallums. The personal name *Calum* is from Columba, and was of old *Maol Caluim* —Devotee of Columba—and, later, Malcolm.

Colgin, about three miles and a half out of Oban, has long been the headquarters of the MacCallums. Tradition states that the chief family of Colgin—consisting at the time of three sons—resolved to leave the parental roof. Their father prepared horses with panniers and gave one to each of the lads. He then sent them away with the direction to take up their residence in whatever place the panniers would fall off the horses. The panniers of the horse of one of them having fallen within the boundaries of the farm, he remained at home. The other two went on their journey, going in different directions. The panniers of the one having fallen in Glenetive, he settled there, and the panniers of the other having fallen at Kilmartin, he made his home in that district. In later years the name was changed to Malcolm.

In 1562 Donald M'Gillespie vic O'Challum was seized in the lands of Poltalloch, and was the lineal ancestor of Neil Malcolm of Poltalloch, who succeeded his cousin, Dugald, in 1787 and died in 1802. John Wingfield Malcolm of Poltalloch was created Lord Malcolm in 1896, and died in 1902. He was succeeded in the estate by his brother, Colonel Edward Donald Malcolm, C.B., R.E.

It would appear that the original tartan of the MacCallums was supplanted by the modern design, called "Malcolm." The old MacCallum tartan had light blue lines where we have red ones in the setting here given.

The general impression is, that this family, having lost trace of the original sett, endeavoured to have it prepared from the recollection of aged natives of Argyllshire, but, as might be expected, the recovery of the old sett shows that marked deviations had been made.

MACCALLUM.

THE CLAN MACDONALD.

War Cry :—" Fraoch Eilean " (" The Heathery Isle ").
Badge :—Fraoch gorm (Common Heath).

THE clan is generally reckoned the oldest and most famous
of Scottish clans, claiming descent from Donald, grandson of Somerled of the Isles, in the twelfth century.
The name Somerled is Norse, *Sumarlidhi,*—that is, mariner.
He died in 1164, and was buried in Saddel Monastery, leaving
three sons—Dugall, Reginald, and Angus.

The southern Isles and a portion of Argyll were divided
among the sons of Sumerled or Somerled in the following
manner : Lorn, Mull, and Jura were given to Dugall ; Kintyre and Islay went to Reginald ; while Bute, with part of
Arran and the roughbounds, extending from Ardnamurchan
to Glenelg, were bequeathed to Angus.

Reginald, the son of Somerled, died in 1207. By Fonia,
daughter of the Earl of Moray, Reginald had three sons—
Donald, Roderick, and Dugall. Donald succeeded his father
in the lordship of south Kintyre, Islay, and other island
possessions ; while Roderick obtained north Kintyre, Bute,
and the land of Garmoran from Ardnamurchan to Glenelg,
all of which formed the possessions of Angus MacSomerled ;
Lochaber passing to the Comyns.

From Donald, son of Reginald, the clan takes its name.
About this time, or shortly after it, fixed patronymics came
into existence in the Highlands, while in the Lowlands the
surnames adopted were generally territorial. The collateral
branches of the House of Somerled after Donald were more or
less independent of one another, and in order to avoid con-
fusion, such patronymics as MacRuairi, MacDugall, Mac-
Alister, and others became fixed. After the middle of the
fourteenth century there is no record of a new patronymic
springing from the House of Somerled. The patronymic of
the Chief is *Mac-Dhòmhnuill-nan-Eilean*—MacDonald of the
Isles.

There is a MacDonald Society, with its headquarters in
Glasgow.

The chiefship of Clan Donald as a whole is left in abeyance,
though each of the three branches (Clanranald, Sleat, Glengarry) has claims to it.

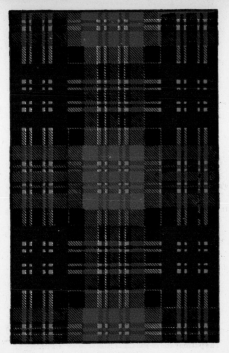

F   CLAN MACDONALD.

MACDONALD OF CLANRANALD.

War Cry :—" Dh' aindeòin co theireadh e " (" Gainsay who dare ").

Badge :—Fraoch gorm (Common Heath).

THE descent of this clan is from John, Lord of the Isles, who married Ami *de* Insulis, and had a son, Ranald—hence the appellation of Clanranald.

Dougall, Chief of Clanranald in the sixteenth century, made himself so obnoxious by cruelties that the tribe slew him ; and then by election the command of the clan and lands was given to Alister Alanson, his uncle, to the exclusion of his sons, who were then young. Alister died in 1530, when his natural son, John of Moydart, was acknowledged as Chief, but for turbulence was lodged in prison by James IV. The Frasers now attempted to reduce the rights he had acquired in favour of Ranald Gallda, or the Stranger, so called from his being fostered by the Frasers. He was a son of Allan Mac-Ruairidh, Chief of Clanranald 1481-1509. Alister Alanson was son of a first marriage. This brought about the battle known as Blar-leine in 1544. Young Ranald was slain, and John of Moydart became eventually the firm friend of Lovat. He died in 1584.

His son, Alan, married a daughter of MacLeod of Harris, and died in 1593. Alan's son, Sir Donald, who was knighted by James VI., died in 1619. Sir Donald's son, John of Clanranald, served in the Wars of Montrose in 1644. He died in old age at Uist in 1670. He was succeeded by his son, John, who died in 1686.

Ranald, who was Chief at the time of 1745, was " out " with the Prince—with a following of 700 men. He lived in exile after Culloden. He was succeeded by his son, John, who died in Edinburgh 1794, and was succeeded by his son, Reginald George MacDonald, eighteenth Chief of Clanranald, who died in 1873. The present representative is Angus R. MacDonald.

The patronymic of the Chief is *Mac Mhic Ailein.*

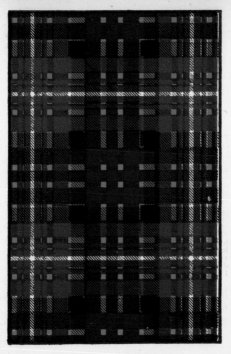

MACDONALD, CLANRANALD.

THE MACDONALDS OF SLEAT.

Badge :—Fraoch gorm (Common Heath).

THE MacDonalds of Sleat are descended from Hugh, son of Alexander, Earl of Ross and Lord of the Isles—hence their patronymic of *Clann Uisdein*, or Children of Hugh. The earliest residence connected with the Barony of Sleat in occupation of *Clann Uisdein* was the fortalice of Dunskaich, lying south of Sleat.

Hugh (I.) of Sleat was thrice married. He died in 1498, and was succeeded by his son, John, who died in 1502. He was succeeded by his brother, Donald Gallach, whose mother was Elizabeth Gunn, a daughter of the Crouner of Caithness, hence the appellation *Gallach*—*i.e.*, a native of Caithness. Donald was murdered by his half-brother in 1506. Donald Gallach had Donald Gruamach and other three sons. Donald Gruamach succeeded his father, and died 1534. He was succeeded by his eldest son, Donald Gorm, who was killed in 1539. He was succeeded by his son, Donald, who was known in history as "*Dòmhnull Gorm Sasunnach*," on account of his having spent part of his minority in England. He died in 1585, and was succeeded by Donald Gorm Mór, his son. He died without issue, and was succeeded by Sir Donald Macdonald, first Baronet of Sleat.

Since the extinction of the direct line of the family of the Isles, in the middle of the sixteenth century, MacDonald of Sleat has always been styled in Gaelic "*Mac-Dhòmhnuill-nan-Eilean*," or MacDonald of the Isles.

The present representative is Sir Alexander Wentworth MacDonald Bosville MacDonald, fourteenth Baronet of Sleat.

MACDONALD, SLEAT.

THE MACDONELLS OF GLENGARRY.

War Cry :—" Creagan-an-fhithich " (" The Raven's Rock ").
Badge :—Fraoch gorm (Common Heath).

THE early history of this family is involved in considerable obscurity, as is indeed that of the other cadet families of the Isles.

John, Lord of the Isles, granted to Reginald a charter of many lands, including lands in Lochaber. The family had also lands in North Morar, and this was possibly the first lands they possessed, for the early representatives of the family are on record as " of Morar and Glengarry."

Alexander, the son of Donald, is referred to in several MS. histories as the first of the MacDonell family who possessed Glengarry ; but the earliest recorded evidence of the actual possession of a MacDonell of the Clanranald branch of the lands of Glengarry is no further back than the year 1496. It is more than probable, however, that for a hundred years prior to this date the family, through a succession of chieftains, occupied the lands of Glengarry. It is interesting to know that it was in the year 1660 that " MacDonell " as a family name in connection with Glengarry was first used, and that in the patent of nobility granted to the grandson and successor of Donald MacAngus.

In the Rising of " the '45 " the MacDonells of Glengarry took an active part. They were present in great force at Falkirk and at Culloden. After the battle of Culloden Old Glengarry was taken prisoner and immured in Edinburgh Castle.

About the beginning of the nineteenth century Alister Ronaldson MacDonell was Chief of Glengarry, and he may truly be called the last representative of the Highland Chief of history. He wore the Highland dress on all occasions, and was invariably accompanied by a body of retainers in full Highland costume. He was accidentally killed in 1828. The present head of the ancient House of Glengarry is Æneas Ranald Westrop M'Donell, **twenty-first** representative and present Chief.

The patronymic of the Chief is *Mac Mhic Alasdair.*

MACDONELL, GLENGARRY.

THE MACDONELLS OF KEPPOCH

War Cry :—" Dia is Naomh Aindrea " (" God and
St. Andrew ").
Badge :—Fraoch Geal (White Heather).

WHEN Angus Og's son, John, Lord of the Isles, came to
apportion his estates between the children of his two
marriages, according to the marriage settlement made
with his second father-in-law, Robert II., the Lordship of
Lochaber was given to the third and youngest son of the
second marriage, *Alastair Carrach*, the first MacDonell of
Keppoch and Garragach. He took an active part in support-
ing the claims of his brother, Donald, Lord of the Isles, to
the Earldom of Ross, with the result that, on the death of
Lord Donald in 1425, the Lordship of Lochaber was forfeited
to the Crown, by whom it was bestowed on a natural son of
the Earl of Mar. This grant was afterwards cancelled, but the
Lordship of Lochaber reverted not to Alastair Carrach, but to
the Lord of the Isles, by whom the lands of Lochaber were
subsequently granted to the Mackintosh Chief, an arrangement
afterwards confirmed by the Crown. The superiority, however, remained with the Lord of the Isles, who restored it to
Alastair Carrach. The latter arrangement was never confirmed
by the Crown, and, on the final forfeiture of the Lordship of
the Isles in 1493, Angus, second MacDonell of Keppoch, had to
maintain his position in Lochaber by his strong right hand.
This he and his successors succeeded in doing for two and a
half centuries. Not until the final downfall of the clan system,
immediately after the battle of Culloden (1746), did Mackintosh become the real Lord, and the erstwhile Lords, the brave
Keppochs, had to yield perforce to the law, recognising that
the day of the sword was gone.

The patronymic of the Chief was *Mac-Mhic Raonuill*, from
Ronald Mor (VII.) of Keppoch ; while the Gaelic designation
of the family is *Clann Mhic Raonuill na Ceapach.*

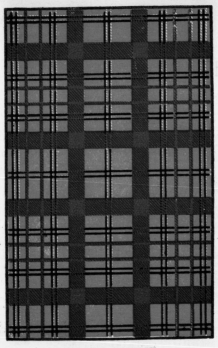

MACDONELL, KEPPOCH

THE CLAN MACDOUGALL.

War Cry :—" Buaidh no bàs " (" Victory or Death ").
Badge :—Fraoch dearg (Bell Heath) ; also Cypress.

FROM Dugall, the eldest son of Somerled of the Isles, is descended this clan. Dugall's mother was Raghnild, sister of Godfred of Man and the Isles. Dugall's son was Duncan of Argyll or Ergadia or Lorn. From his father Duncan got the cradle of the clan—Lorn—and we have " Duncan of Argyll " on record as early as 1244. Duncan's son was King Ewin of Argyll, who refused to join Haco in 1263. King Ewin's son was Alexander of Lorn, who died about 1310. He was succeeded by his son, John, the obstinate opponent of Robert the Bruce, who gained possession of the " Brooch of Lorn." John was seized in 1318 and imprisoned in Dumbarton for his opposition to Bruce. He was set at liberty on the death of Bruce, and all his property restored to him.

John was succeeded by his son, John, about 1354. John's daughter, Jonete, was his heir, and in 1358 she conveyed Lorn to Sir Robert Steward of Innermeath, and so we read of " John Steward, Lord of Lorn," in 1394. In 1457 John Stewart, Lord of Lorn, granted to John MacAlan, called " McCowle " (MacDougall), and to John Keir, his son, twenty-nine merklands of Kerraray, six merks of Dunolly.

John MacAlan's descendants held the lands of Dunolly undisturbed till 1715, when they were forfeited on account of the then Chief, Iain Ciar, having been present, with 200 of his clansmen, at Sheriffmuir. Iain Ciar died about the middle of the eighteenth century, and was succeeded by his son, Alexander, who was succeeded by his son, Patrick, who was succeeded by his son, John, afterwards Sir John MacDougall, Admiral, K.C.B. The Admiral died in 1864, and was succeeded by his son, Alexander, a Captain in the army. He died in 1867, and was succeeded by his brother, Lieutenant-Colonel Charles Allan MacDougall, who died in 1896. He was succeeded by his brother, Henry Robert MacDougall, Deputy Surgeon-General, Bombay Army, who was succeeded by his son, Alexander James MacDougall, C.M.G., Lieut.-Col. R.A.M.C., of MacDougall and Dunollie, Oban.

The seat of the Chief is Dunollie.

There is a Clan MacDougall Society in Lorn, with branches in Edinburgh and Glasgow.

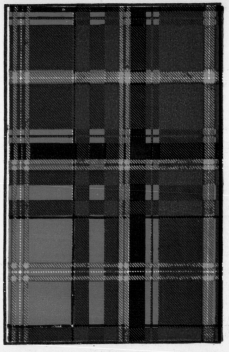

MACDOUGALL.

THE CLAN MACDUFF.

Badge :—Bocsa (Boxwood) or Lus nan cnàimhseag (Red Whortleberry).

MACDUFF is the patronymic of the first or Celtic Earls of Fife. Ethelred, son of King Malcolm Canmore, is the first recorded Earl of Fife. He was also Abbot of Dunkeld. Constantine was Earl of Fife in the early days of David's reign, and, dying about 1129, was succeeded by Gillimichel Mak-duf, or Son of Duff or Dufagan, probably his brother. The origin of these three Earls is unknown, but it is a remarkable fact that the genealogies given for King Lulach and King Macbeth are headed " Genealogy of Clan Duff."

Certain privileges were accorded to Clan Duff, and these are referred to in an Act of 1384. These privileges were: First, that they should seat the king in his Royal chair on his coronation day ; second, that they should lead the vanguard in every Royal battle ; and third, a remission for homicide on a fixed payment, with sanctuary at Cross MacDuff, which stood to the north of Newburgh.

Gillimichel MacDuff was succeeded by his son, Duncan, and he again by his son, Duncan, fifth Earl. Duncan's son, Malcolm, was succeeded by his nephew, Malcolm, who left two sons—his successor, Colban, and MacDuff—his Christian name is not given—who was the primary cause of John Baliol's rebellion against Edward I. Duncan, the eleventh Earl, died about 1353, leaving an only daughter, and the line of the Celtic Earls of Fife came to an end.

The Duffs of Banffshire claim descent from the Earls of Fife. It is quite possible that David Duff of Muldavit, in Banffshire (1401), was a descendant of the Earls of Fife, as was claimed, and that his descendant was William Duff, Lord Braco (1725), who received in 1759 the titles of Viscount Mac-Duff and Earl of Fife in the Peerage of Ireland. James Duff, the fourth Earl, was raised to the British Peerage in 1827 as Baron Fife.

The present representative is H.H. Princess Alexandra Victoria Alberta Edwina Louise, who succeeded her father as Duchess of Fife in 1912.

MACDUFF.

THE CLAN MACEWEN.

THIS clan, though now extinct, was of considerable importance at one time. Its habitat was in Cowal. The MacEwens were known as *Clann Eóghain na h-Oitrich*—the MacEwens of Otter—and as late as 1750 there stood on a rocky point on the coast of Lochfyne, about a mile below the church at Kilfinnan, the vestige of a building called *Caisteal Mhic Eóghain*—MacEwen's Castle. The MacEwens were closely allied to the MacLachlans and the MacNeills. In the twelfth century the Lamonts, the MacLachlans, and the MacEwens were in possession of the greater part of Cowal.

The earliest Chief of whom we have any record flourished about the thirteenth century. He was succeeded by Severn (II.) of Otter. About 1315 Gillespie (V.) of Otter assumed the chiefship. From this date there were four Chiefs—Ewen (VI.), John (VII.), Walter (VIII.), and Swene (IX.), the last of the Otter Chiefs.

In 1431–32 this Swene granted a charter of certain lands of Otter to Duncan, son of Alexander Campbell. In 1432 he resigned the Barony of Otter to James I., but received it anew from the King, with remainder to Celestine Campbell, son and heir of Duncan Campbell of Lochow. After Swene's death, King James in 1493 confirmed the grant to Archibald, Earl of Argyll, as heir to his father, Colin. In 1575 another Archibald Campbell appears in a charter as " of the Otter," and in the Act of 1587 a Campbell is entered as " the Laird of Otter."

After the middle of the fifteenth century the Barony and estates of Otter passed and gave title to a branch of the Campbells, and the MacEwens became a scattered clan. As a necessity of the times some of them sought new alliances. Some appear to have followed MacLachlan of MacLachlan, and others sought protection as " men " of the Earl of Argyll. Some joined the Campbells of Craignish, while colonies were formed in the Lennox country in Dumbartonshire, and in Galloway.

The MacEwens were hereditary bards to the Campbells.

MACEWEN.

THE CLAN MACFARLANE.

War Cry :—" Loch Slòigh " (" The Loch of the Host ").
Badge :—Muileag (Cranberry), Oireag or Foighreag
(Cloudberry).

DESCENDED from the ancient Celtic Earls of Lennox, the
MacFarlanes occupied the land forming the western shore
of Loch Lomond from Tarbet upwards. From Loch
Sloy, a small sheet of water near the foot of Ben Voirlich, they
took their war cry of *Loch Slòigh.* The ancestor of the clan
was Gilchrist, brother of Maldowen, the third Earl of Lennox.
Gilchrist's grandson was Bartholomew, which in Gaelic is
Parlan, from whom the clan are designed—the letters " Ph "
in *MacPhàrlain* sounding like F in Gaelic.

In 1373 the death of Donald, the sixth and last of the old
Earls of Lennox, without male issue, left the Chief of the Clan
MacFarlane the male representative of the old Lennox family.
The claim was disputed, and ultimately the Earldom of Lennox
was conferred on Sir John Stewart of Darnley, who married
Elizabeth, one of the daughters of the last Earl of Lennox of
the old line. The resistance of the MacFarlanes to the *Stewart*
Earls of Lennox would appear to have been the beginning of
the end of their destruction as a clan. That the MacFarlanes
were not entirely deprived of their territory was in consequence
of the marriage of Andrew, head of one of the cadet branches,
to the daughter of John Stewart, Earl of Lennox. By this
marriage Andrew MacFarlane obtained possession of the clan
territory of Arrochar. His son, Sir John MacFarlane, assumed
in 1493 the designation of Captain of the Clan MacFarlane, the
clan refusing him the higher title of Chief, seeing that he was
not the representative of the ancient Chiefs of the clan, which
family had become extinct in the male line some time previously
to this.

The Clan MacFarlane became a " broken clan " towards the
end of the sixteenth century. The last descendant of the Chiefs
is said to have gone to America at the end of the eighteenth
century, and there does not seem to be any trace of his descendants, so that the clan is virtually landless and chiefless.

G   MACFARLANE.

THE MACFIES OR MACPHEES.

Badge :—Darag (Oak) or Dearca fithich (Crowberry).

THE oldest form of this surname is MacDuffie (*MacDubh-sithe*), and it is so written in a charter of 1463. The original home of the clan was Colonsay, of which they were in possession till about the middle of the seventeenth century.

Murroch was the name of the MacDuffie Chief in 1531. In 1609 Donald Macfie of Colonsay was one of the twelve Chiefs and gentlemen who met the Bishop of the Isles, the King's representative, at Iona, when the celebrated "Statutes of Icolmkill" were enacted. In 1615 Malcolm Macfie of Colonsay joined Sir James MacDonald of Islay after his escape from the Castle of Edinburgh, and was one of the principal leaders in his subsequent rebellions. He and eighteen others were delivered by Coll Kitto MacDonald (*Colla Ciotach*) to the Earl of Argyll, by whom he was brought before the Privy Council—for we learn that in 1623 Coll Kitto was delated for the murder of the umquhile Malcolm Macfee. From this period Colonsay seems to have gone into the possession of the MacDonalds, and afterwards to the Duke of Argyll, who exchanged Colonsay and Oronsay for Crerar, in South Knapdale, with Donald MacNeill, two of whose descendants have shed great lustre upon Colonsay—in law and in diplomacy—Lord Colonsay and his brother, the Right Hon. Sir John MacNeill, G.C.B.

On the death of Sir John Carstairs MacNeill, K.C.M.G., V.C., in 1904, the Island was purchased by Lord Strathcona.

When the Macphees were dispossessed of their original inheritance they became a "broken clan," lost their independence, and so were obliged to rank under more powerful clans. The greater part followed the MacDonalds of Islay, while others settled in the country of the Camerons under Lochiel, where they were distinguished for their bravery.

MACFIE.

THE CLAN MACGILLIVRAY.

War Cry :—" Dunmaglass."
Badge :—Lus nam braoileag (Red Whortleberry).

THE MacGillivrays, one of the oldest septs of Clan Chattan, are known in Gaelic as *Clann Mhic Gillebhràth*, and, according to the Croy MS. history, it is said that about the year 1268 " Gillivray, the progenitor of Clan vic Gillivray, took protection and dependence for himself and posterity of this Farquhard Mackintosh (fifth of Mackintosh, who was killed in 1274, aged thirty-six).''

It is more than likely that the MacGillivrays came originally from the West Coast—probably from Mull—where we find them centuries ago, and where they are still to be found in considerable numbers. Those of them who came northward must have settled at Dunmaglass many centuries ago.

Duncan MacGillivray, who flourished about 1500, is regarded as *first* of Dunmaglass. In 1609, when the famous Clan Chattan Bond of Union was signed, the MacGillivray Chief was a minor, and so the Bond was signed by three representatives of the clan on behalf of the heir.

The MacGillivrays took an active part in the Rising of 1715. The Laird and his brother, William, were Captain and Lieutenant respectively in the Clan Chattan Regiment. The clan was also " out " in " the '45," and were led at Culloden by Alexander, their Chief, who fell, fighting, at a well on the battlefield, which still bears his name.

About the end of the eighteenth century the estate was in a very embarrassed condition, and the Chief (William) got a captaincy in the Gordon Regiment. He died in 1783, and was succeeded by his son, John Lachlan MacGillivray, who possessed the estate for nearly seventy years. He died in 1852 " possessed of some £40,000 of money, which was destined by will, including a year's rent to all his tenants ; also the heritable estates undisposed of, but free and unburdened.'' A severe competition arose as to all the estates except one, with the result that the patrimonial estates were dispersed.

The present Chief is Mr. J. W. MacGillivray of Dunmaglass.

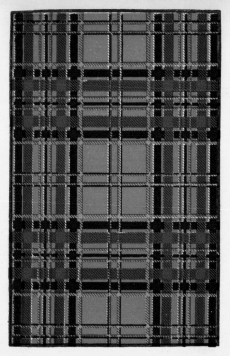

MACGILLIVRAY.

THE CLAN MACGREGOR.

War Cry :—" Ard Choille " (" High Wood ").
Badge :—Giuthas (Pine Tree).

THE ancient motto of this clan—*Is rioghail mo dhream*—claims for them Royal descent. The earliest possessions of the clan were in Glenorchy, and they made their graves in a small chapel of Dysart, near Dalmally, from about the fourteenth century. When Highland lairds began to accept Crown charters for their lands, the MacGregors would have none of them, and strove to assert *Còir a' chlaidheimh*, or right of the sword. This brought them into sharp conflict with the authorities, as well as with their neighbours, who were anxious to seize their possessions, and had no scruples in carrying to the ears of the Sovereign the worst possible accounts of the MacGregors. Throughout their hardships they remained loyal to the King.

The lands of Glenorchy passed away by the marriage of an heiress, after which MacGregor of Glenstray exercised the chiefship for several centuries. In 1603 a conflict took place between the Clan Gregor and the Colquhouns of Luss, who had been induced to execute a commission of " fire and sword," issued by King James VI., against the dreaded clan. The battle was fought in Glenfruin in 1603, and, although the result was a victory for the MacGregors, the authorities were so incensed that they afterwards aimed at the annihilation of the whole clan. Alexander MacGregor, the brave Chief, was executed at Edinburgh, with many of his followers, in 1604.

MacGregor of Roro, in Glenlyon, is the oldest cadet of the clan, and is mentioned early in the fifteenth century. The last holding of the property was sold in 1760.

MacGregor of Glengyle was an old cadet, but certainly junior to Roro.

The name MacGregor was absolutely proscribed after Glenfruin under the most severe penalties, but an Act to annul the suppression of the name was passed in Parliament in November 1774.

The present Chief is Sir Malcolm MacGregor, fifth Baronet, C.B., C.M.G.

MACGREGOR.

THE MACINNESES.

Badge:—Cuileann (Holly).

BEING of common origin with the Clan MacDonald, the Macinneses are recognised as a sept of "the premier clan." The name Angus (in Gaelic, *Aonghas*, hence—*Clann Aonghais*—Children of Angus), whether we regard it as a personal or as a place-name, is very ancient in Scotland. The first to bear it was the brother of Loarn and Fergus, the earliest Kings of the Dalriadic Scots.

According to Skene, "the Cineal Angus possessed Islay and Jura, and consisted of 430 houses."

Skene and other historians agree that the oldest inhabitants of Morvern, Ardgour, and Lochaber consisted of two clans, the MacGillivrays and the Macinneses, who were of the same race; and, as Skene remarks, "as there is a very old traditionary connection between the *Clann-a'-Mhaigster* (Mac-Masters), or Macinnes of Ardgour, and several of the clans descended from Anradan MacGillebride, it seems to establish the identity of this tribe with the old MacGillivrays of Morvern."

The seat of the Chief of Clan Macinnes was at Kinlochaline in Morvern. There is a tradition that, after returning from an expedition in which the Macinneses had rendered signal service, the Chief of the clan was addressed thus by the Lord of the Isles: "My blessing on you, Chief of Kinlochaline! while MacDonald is in power, Macinnes shall be in favour."

The Macinneses were hereditary bowman to the Chiefs of the Clan Mackinnon—evidently a bodyguard. The first of these, and also one of the first who migrated from Morvern to Skye, was a famous warrior-archer, known as *Niall a' Bhogha* —Neil of the Bow. Some of his descendants are said to be still in Skye.

The Macinneses are eligible for membership in the Clan Donald Society.

MACINNES.

THE CLAN MACINTYRE.

War Cry :—" Cruachan " (A mountain near Loch Awe).
Badge :—Fraoch gorm (Common Heath).

I T is generally agreed that the Macintyres are an offshoot
from Clan Donald. It is a well-known fact that the Macintyres of Glenoe, Lochetive, occupied these lands for a
period of 500 or 600 years prior to 1806. The tenure by which
they held Glenoe from the Campbells of Glenorchy, afterwards
of Breadalbane, was a payment annually in summer of a snowball and a white fatted calf. The snowball could easily be
got at the back of Cruachan, and as they always kept a white
cow or two, a white calf was also procurable. This arrangement continued till about the beginning of the eighteenth
century, when the tenant of Glenoe, at the time, foolishly
agreed to the payment being commuted to money, which
then became rent, and was increased to so large a sum that
the Macintyres could not pay it and make a comfortable living,
and in 1806 they were under the necessity of parting with the
home of their fathers.

There was a strong colony of Macintyres resident for many
generations at the village of Cladich, Loch Awe, where they
carried on an extensive weaving industry.

A branch of the clan were dependents of the Campbells of
Craignish, and are mentioned in 1612 as having given a bond
of manrent to Campbell of Barrichbyan.

There were Macintyres in Badenoch who were attached to
the Clan Chattan. In 1496 these Macintyres were, by William,
thirteenth Chief of Mackintosh, admitted as a sept of the Clan
Chattan. A family of Macintyres were hereditary pipers to
Menzies of Menzies, while another family were hereditary
pipers to MacDonald of Clan Ranald.

The Macintyres fought under the banner of the Stewarts of
Appin in 1745.

MACINTYRE.

THE CLAN MACKAY.

War Cry :—" Bratach bhàn Chlann Aoidh " (" The White
   Banner of the Mackays ").
Badge :—Seasgan or Cuilc (Reed Grass).

THIS clan is anciently known as Clan Morgan, and the
Mackays of the North claim to be descended from the
common ancestor of the Forbeses and Urquharts. About
1608 they adopted Lord Forbes's Arms with cadet differences.
In the eleventh century (see *Book of Deer*) the Clan Morgan and
their *Tòiseach* or Chief granted lands to the Abbey of Deer.
The clan are also called *Clann Aoidh*; the Lowland form is
Mackie and the Irish Magee. There are at least two clans
Mackay—an Argyllshire and a Sutherlandshire clan. The
Argyllshire Mackays are to be found at an early date in Islay
and Kintyre; while the Sutherlandshire clan is, as stated
above, regarded as of common origin with the Forbeses.

The first historic Chief of the clan was Angus Du, who
flourished 1380–1429. He was an old man when the fierce
battle of Drumnacoub was fought in 1429, and the clan was
led by Iain Abereigh, who gained a great victory.

In 1642 Lord Reay sold Strathnaver to the Earl of Sutherland, and during the chiefship of Eric, seventh Lord Reay
(1797–1847), the remaining portions of the estate had to be sold,
so that the Mackays of the North, as a clan, are landless.

The Mackays of the South were powerful in Islay and Kintyre, and fought under the banner of the Lord of the Isles.
The earliest Gaelic charter extant was granted by Donald, Lord
of the Isles, to Brian Vicar Mackay, Islay, in 1408.

The present Chief of the clan is the Right Hon. Æneas
Alexander Mackay, thirteenth Baron Reay of Reay in the
Peerage of Scotland, Baron Reay of Durness in that of the
United Kingdom, and Baron Mackay of Ophemert in Holland.

The Clan Mackay Society was founded in 1806 and resus-
citated in 1888. Its headquarters are in Glasgow.

MACKAY.

THE CLAN MACKENZIE.

War Cry :—" Tulach Ard " (A mountain in Kintail).
Badge :—Cuileann (Holly).

THE MacKenzies were vassals of the Earls of Ross, and little or nothing is known of their history until the forfeiture of the last Earl. Their first charter is about the first forfeiture of the Island Lord—1463. The first Chief mentioned is Kenneth Mor (1427), who had a following of 2000 men.

After the final forfeiture of the Lord of the Isles (Earl of Ross) the MacKenzies rapidly increased their influence, and acquired large possessions in Ross-shire. Kenneth MacKenzie of Kintail was knighted by James VI. His son and successor was, in 1609, raised to the Peerage under the title of Lord MacKenzie of Kintail. Colin, second Lord, received the additional dignity of the Earldom of Seaforth in 1623.

The Earl of Seaforth died without male issue in 1784. The estates and the chiefship passed to his cousin, Colonel Thomas Frederick Humberston MacKenzie. The last Earl of Seaforth died in 1815. The chiefship of the clan then passed to the MacKenzies of Allangrange. James F. MacKenzie of Allangrange died 15th August 1907, and was succeeded by Mrs. Beatrice Anna Fraser MacKenzie of Allangrange in Ross-shire.

There are many distinguished cadet branches of the MacKenzies, and at least four Baronetcies are held by members of the clan—those of Gairloch, 1703; Coul, 1673; Tarbet, 1628; and Scatwell, 1703.

In 1745 the effective strength of the Clan MacKenzie was estimated at 2500 men.

The seat of the Chief of the clan was at Brahan Castle, in East Ross. The property is now owned by Col. James Alexander Francis Humberston Stewart-Mackenzie of Seaforth.

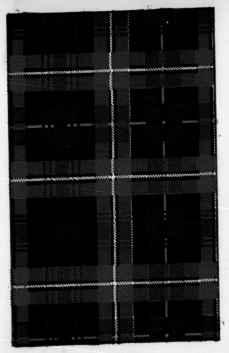

MACKENZIE.

THE CLAN MACKINLAY.

THERE can be little doubt the habitat of this clan was in the Lennox district, where we find them yet in considerable numbers. The oldest account of them is given by Buchanan of Auchmar, 1723. He asserts that the chief sept of the Lennox Mackinlays were descended from Buchanan of Drumikill. After mentioning that the Risks are the first cadets of the Drumikill family, he says: "The second cadets of this kin are the Mackinlays, so named from a son of Drumikill called Finlay; those lately in Blairnyle and about Balloch are of this sort, as also those in Bamachra and above the Water of Finn, in Luss parish. The Mackinlays in some other parts of these parishes are MacFarlanes.

Like so many Lennox clans, notably their far-off cousins of the Clan MacAuslane, some of the Mackinlays no doubt went over to Ireland at the time of the "plantations" in the seventeenth century. Hence come the Mackinlays and Macginlays of Ireland, and latterly of America.

It is a common mistake to regard the clan ancestor as *Fionnlagh Mor*, progenitor of the Farquharsons of Braemar. The Farquharsons as a clan are called in Gaelic *Clann Fhionnlaigh*, but the surname *MacFhionnlaigh* has never come to be used in English dress. In fact, the surname has been constantly Farquharson, and there were no Mackinlays at all in Braemar or its vicinity.

The small Clan Finlayson of Lochalsh are known in Gaelic as *Clann Fhionnlaigh*, and they, too, claim a traditional descent from the Clan Finlay of Braemar.

It is probable the name Mackinlay embraces some of the Macleay clan. Some of the modern Mackinlays insist on accenting the "lay" of the name.

H   MACKINLAY.

THE CLAN MACKINNON.

War Cry :—" Cuimhnich bàs Ailpein " (" Remember the death of Alpin.").

Badge :—Giuthas (Pine Tree).

THE older forms of this clan surname show it to be Fingon, for in 1409 Lachlan MacFingon, *vir nobilis* (*i.e.*, a gentleman), witnessed a charter of the Lord of the Isles to Hector Maclean of Duart. The original habitat of the clan was Mull, where they held lands under the Lords of the Isles. They had also possessions in Strathardale, Skye, as early as 1594. The Mackinnons were closely associated with Iona in the fifteenth century, and John Mackinnon was the last Abbot.

In 1503 Mackinnon of that Ilk is mentioned, among other Chiefs, to take action against Lachlan Maclean of Duart and Lochiel, forfeited for treason.

Ewen, who was Chief of the clan in the sixteenth century, received from the King a charter of the twenty merklands of Meysness (Misnish), in Mull, and the twenty merklands of Strathardale, in Skye.

The clan was " out " in the year 1745, followed the Prince to England, and fought at Culloden ; their old Chief was taken, and, after long imprisonment, died in 1756, leaving two sons and a daughter.

Charles, his son, found the estates so burdened with debt that he had to part with them, and Strathaird, the last of the clan lands, held in unbroken succession for 450 years, passed from the clan in 1791. Charles left an only son, John, the last of his line, who succeeded to nothing but the chiefship. He died in 1808, and the chiefship passed to the descendants of Donald, son of Lachlan Mor.

The present Chief is Major F. A. Mackinnon, B.A.

There is a Clan Mackinnon Society in Glasgow, with a branch in London. *Memoirs of Clan Fingon* was published in 1899.

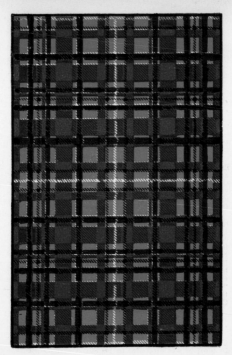

MACKINNON.

THE CLAN MACKINTOSH.

War Cry :—" Loch Mòigh " (" Loch of the Plain "), in an island
of which the former Chiefs had their stronghold.
Badge :—Bocsa (Boxwood) or Lus nam braoileag
(Red Whortleberry)

THE Mackintoshes form the leading sept of the Clan Chattan. The first real chief-of-line was Malcolm Mackintosh (1430–64). The clan lands stretched from Petty to Lochaber inclusive, but none were held directly from the Crown. His relations with the Lord of the Isles, or Earls of Ross, were cordial, and his son, Duncan, married Flora, the Earl's daughter.

William, sixth Chief, was the first Mackintosh Chief to get into difficulties with Huntly, Lord-Lieutenant of the North and Sheriff of Inverness-shire. He was tried in Aberdeen for conspiring against Huntly's life, and by a packed jury found guilty. He was executed at Strathbogie 1550. The estates, with compensation for the murder, were held for his heir through the powerful influence of Moray and other relatives.

For the next two hundred years the clan was engaged in feuds with the Gordons, the Camerons, and the MacDonells of Keppoch. In 1678 Mackintosh got the usual " fire and sword " commission, but it was not till 1688 that he could get his friends and clansmen to help him. These, with a company of Regulars under MacKenzie of Suddie, fought with the Mac-Donells at Mulroy and were defeated. This was the last clan battle. Lachlan, who was Chief from 1660, died in 1704, and was succeeded by his son, Lachlan, who took a gallant part in " the '45." He died, childless, in 1731, and for a hundred years thereafter no son succeeded a father among the Mackintosh Chiefs.

Angus (XIII.) got over " the '45 " period by a half-hearted support of King George ; while his wife, " Colonel Anne," and the clan took the field for Prince Charlie.

Angus, who was Chief from 1827 to 1833, broke the Spell or Curse of Moy, and was succeeded by his son, Alexander. Dying in 1861, he was succeeded by his son, Alexander Æneas, who died in 1875. His brother, Alfred Donald, succeeded him, and is the present holder of the title.

The seat of the Chief is Moy Hall.

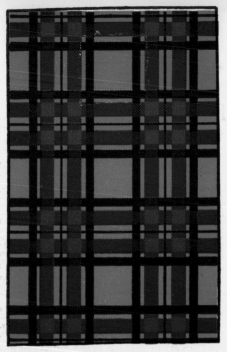

MACKINTOSH.

MACKINTOSH OF MACKINTOSH
(CHIEF OF CLAN CHATTAN).

Badge :—Bocsa (Boxwood) or Lus nam braoileag
(Red Whortleberry).

THE Chief of Clan Chattan derives his name from the Gaelic term *Tòiseach*, a word latterly translated as "thane," and even "bailie," or "baron bailie," or "steward." The particular "thane" from which Mackintosh gets his name is doubtless the thanedom of Rothiemurchus, "My *native* country," as Lachlan Mor, the Chief, pathetically calls it in 1569, when the Mackintoshes were forced to part with it.

The historical Clan Chattan was a confederation really, and the Bond of 1609 gives us the real components. These were : Mackintoshes, Macphersons, Macqueens, MacBeans, Macleans of Dochgarroch, MacGillivrays, Shaws, and also MacPhails. The Farquharsons of Braemar are an early offshoot, and sporadic names like Gow, Gillanders, and Clark are claimed. There seems to be good reason to believe that Davidson also formed part of the Macpherson clan, although the whole name of Davidson is of much wider connotation than attaches to the Clan Chattan. The name Cattanach interchanges with Mackintosh in the oldest records. About 1600 the habitat of these septs mostly lay thus : Mackintoshes, all over the Clan Chattan country ; Macphersons, in Badenoch and in Strathnairn, Petty, etc., indeed, it may be questioned if the original "Parson" was not from the vicinity of Inverness ; Macqueens, in Upper Strathdearn ; MacBeans, in Dores and thereabouts ; Shaws, in Rothiemurchus and Strathnairn ; MacGillivrays, in Strathnairn.

The name of the clan—Chattan—is derived from an ancestor called "*Gillie-cattan*"—Devotee of St. Cattan (Little Cat)—but his date and history are both unknown to true history. The Clan Chattan has no connection, either in name or history, with the "*Catti of Cataobh*," or Sutherland.

The Chiefs of some clans wore separate tartans from their men, which accounts for there being two tartans under the name of Mackintosh.

MACKINTOSH, CHIEF.

THE CLAN MACLACHLAN.

Badge :—Caorunn (Mountain Ash or Rowan).

THE MacLachlans are believed to have been in possession of Strathlachlan, in Argyllshire, since the eleventh century. At one time they owned extensive lands in Argyllshire, which are now reduced to the Barony of MacLachlan or Strathlachlan. Their intermarriages are given in the MS. of 1450, and are with such families as those of the Lords of the Isles, the King of Kerry, etc. In 1292 the lands of Gileskel MacLachlan were included in the Sheriffdom of Argyll or Lorn, erected in that year by King John Baliol. From Gileskel there is no difficulty in tracing the direct line down to the present day.

The MacLachlans threw in their fate with Prince Charles, and it says much for the popularity of Lachlan MacLachlan, who was then Chief, that he was able to make his way with his men from the very centre of Argyll and join the Prince in the North, despite the fact that he was surrounded by Campbells and other keen partisans of the House of Hanover. MacLachlan was appointed A.D.C. to the Prince, and was killed at Culloden. The lands were attainted after " the '45," but the next heir, Robert, was granted possession by a judgment of the Court, dated 28th November 1749.

The three original tribes of Cowal are said to have been the Lamonts, the MacEwens, and the MacLachlans. The Lamonts and MacLachlans intermarried several times.

The oldest cadet of the clan are the MacLachlans of Coruanan, Lochaber, who held the position of hereditary standard-bearers to the Camerons of Lochiel.

The seat of John MacLachlan, Esq. (twenty-third), of that Ilk is Castle Lachlan, Strathlachlan, Loch Fyne.

MACLACHLAN.

THE CLAN MACLAREN.

War Cry :—" Creag an Tuirc " (" The Boar's Rock ").
Badge :—Buaidh-chraobh, na Labhras (Laurel).

IT is most likely that the MacLarens are descended from
Laurentius or St. Lawrence. In Gaelic they are called
Clann mhic Labhrainn, and in English the surname is
sometimes written MacLaurin. The clan is an ancient one,
and in the earlier period of their history were possessed of
considerable influence. From various causes they gradually
declined in importance and strength.

They signed the Ragman Roll of 1296, compelled for the
time, like many other clans, to swear fealty to King Edward I.,
and they did so under three branches, represented by Maurice
of Tiree, Conan of Balquhidder, and Laurin of Ardveche
(Lochearnside).

An interesting and romantic episode in their history is their
alliance—offensive and defensive, it may be called—with the
Stewarts of Appin. It arose out of the love-at-first-sight
attachment of the third last of the " Stewart " Lords of Lorn
in the fifteenth century for the beautiful daughter of Mac-
Laurin of Ardveche, and their subsequent marriage and legiti-
mation of their son, Dugald, who became the founder of the
famous Stewarts of Appin.

In local history the clan had their full share of clan feuds
with their neighbours—the Buchanans, Campbells, and Mac-
Gregors. On one occasion, in the twelfth century, a pitched
battle took place in Strathyre over an insult to a MacLaren,
when they practically annihilated the Buchanans of Leny.

It is interesting to note that it was in connection with
some legal proceedings anent the MacLaurins of Invernentie
that Sir Walter Scott made his first acquaintance with the
Highlands.

The clan is at present landless and chiefless.

MACLAREN.

THE MACLAINES OF LOCHBUIE.

Badge :—Blaeberry.

THE Lochbuie Maclaines are descended from Hector Reaganach, brother of Lachlan Lùbanach, the progenitor of the Macleans of Duart. Hector Reaganach received the lands of Lochbuie from John, first Lord of the Isles. According to tradition, these lands were held in possession by a chieftain named MacFadyen. Hector had several sons. Tearlach (Charles) was the progenitor of *Clan Thearlaich* of Dochgarroch, or the Macleans of the North. The second Chief of Lochbuie was Murdoch Roy, son of Hector Reaganach.

When John Og (V.) of Lochbuie died he was succeeded by his son, Murchadh Gearr, or Short Murdoch, about 1494. His uncle, Murdoch of Scallasdale, seized the estate and tried to keep possession of it. Murdoch Gearr fled to Ireland but soon returned, supported by a strong bodyguard. He made himself known to his nurse, who helped him to gain possession of the Castle of Lochbuie. Shortly afterwards he defeated Murdoch of Scallasdale at Grulin.

The Maclaines served with Graham of Claverhouse, Viscount Dundee, and also under Montrose with their kinsmen, the Macleans of Duart. Hector Maclaine of Lochbuie, with 300 men, on his march to join Dundee, was attacked by five troops of horse sent by the enemy to intercept him. The parties met, and, after a severe fight, Lochbuie put the horse to flight and killed the commander.

Donald (XXI.) of Lochbuie was born in 1816. He went to Batavia, in Java, entered into business as a merchant, and amassed quite a fortune. He purchased the estate of Lochbuie from those who held it for debt, and thus, fortunately, saved it from passing out of the hands of the descendants of Hector Reaganach. His grandson, Kenneth Douglas Lorne Maclaine, M.C., Major 15th Hussars, Special Reserve, is the present representative of the Maclaines of Lochbuie.

MACLAINE OF LOCHBUIE.

THE MACLEANS OF DUART.

War Cries :—"Beatha no Bàs" ("Life or Death") and "Fear eil' airson Eachainn"("Another for Hector"). Used alternately.
Badges :—Dearca fithich (Crowberry), used by Duart, Brolas, Pennycross, Drimnin ; Cuileann (Holly), used by Maclean of Ardgour, Coll, Dochgarroch, and Macleans of the North.

THE progenitor of this clan was *Gilleain-na-Tuaigh*, or Gillean of the Battle Axe, who flourished in the thirteenth century. The axe which rendered him famous is represented in the Maclean crest. In 1294 we find "Gillemoir Mackilyn" signing Ragman Roll.

John, son of Gillemoir, had two sons, Lachlan Lùbanach, progenitor of the Macleans of Duart, and Eachann Reaganach, the progenitor of the Maclaines of Lochbuie. These brothers lived during the reign of Robert II., and appear first as followers of the Lord of Lorn ; but some dispute having arisen, they left him and followed MacDonald, Lord of the Isles, who received them with great favour. Lachlan Lùbanach afterwards married Margaret, daughter of the Lord of the Isles, and was appointed by him his Lieutenant-General in time of war.

The Clan Maclean acquired extensive possessions in Mull, Tiree, Coll, Islay, Morvern, and Lochaber. On the forfeiture of the last Lord of the Isles, the Macleans assumed independence, and appear to have gradually risen on the ruins of that great clan. Towards the close of the sixteenth century the MacDonalds appear to have united for the purpose of effectively crushing the rising power of the Macleans.

The direct line of Duart became extinct early in the seventeenth century, and the honours of that family devolved upon Allan Maclean of Brolas, the next cadet in succession. The present Chief of the Clan Maclean is Colonel Sir Fitzroy Donald Maclean, K.C.B., tenth Baronet, of Duart, Morvern, and Brolas.

Duart Castle occupies the verge of a high cliff on the coast of Mull. It is of great antiquity, and is a square tower with walls of enormous thickness.

There is a Clan Maclean Society in Glasgow.

MACLEAN OF DUART.

THE CLAN MACLEOD.

Badge :—Aitionn (Juniper).

THE original progenitor of both branches of MacLeod family was Leod. He was son of Olave, King of Man. Born early in the thirteenth century, he married the daughter of MacRailt, Armuinn. She was heiress of Dunvegan. By her he had two sons—Tormod, the ancestor of the MacLeods of Harris ; and Torquil, the ancestor of the MacLeods of Lewis.

The Lewis MacLeods (Siol Torquil) became extinct in the direct line in the sixteenth century. The heiress of that branch was wedded to one of the MacKenzies of Seaforth. After the extinction of the direct line of Siol Torquil, the chiefship of this branch of the Clan MacLeod passed to the senior cadet, MacLeod of Raasay. When this family became extinct, in the early part of the nineteenth century, the head-ship of the family passed to MacLeod of Cadboll.

Siol Tormod, though no longer owners of the large terri-tories of bygone days, still retain a good portion of the old clan lands. The seat of the Chief is still at Dunvegan Castle, Skye. It has been truly said that Dunvegan Castle is a fine old place, " combining the romance of the ninth with the comfort of the twentieth century." In it are preserved count-less relics of the past.

The MacCrimmons, most famous of Highland pipers, were for centuries the pipers of the MacLeods. In modern times the most famous members of the clan have been the scions of the MacLeods of Morvern ; but all over the world are to be found cadets of the family—MacLeods of Gesto, of Meidle and Glendale, of Drynoch, of Talisker, of Bernera, of Hamer, of Greshornish, of Ulinish, of Dalvey, of Orbost, of Rigg, of Assynt, of Geanies, and many others.

There is a Clan MacLeod Society in Edinburgh.

The present (twenty-fourth) Chief of the clan is Sir Reginald MacLeod, a brother of the former Chief.

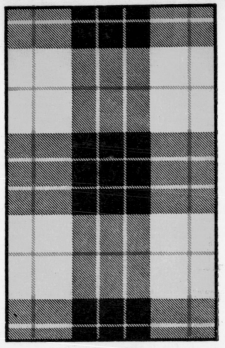

MACLEOD.

THE CLAN MACMILLAN.

Badge :—Cuileann (Holly).

THE origin of this clan is difficult to determine. It is pretty generally believed that they are of ecclesiastical origin. In the Highlands an individual member of the clan is referred to by Gaelic-speaking people as *MacMhaoilein* or *MacGillemhaoil*—*maol* being the Gaelic for bald or tonsured.

A branch of the clan is found at Loch Arkaig, in Lochaber, at an early period. They were among the loyal followers of Lochiel. From Loch Arkaig the clan, as tradition says, were removed by Malcolm IV. (1153-65) and placed on the Crown lands of Loch Tay in Perthshire. The estate of Lawers belonged to them. From Lawers they were driven in the fourteenth century. Some of them migrated southward to Knapdale, on the Argyllshire coast, and others to Galloway. The Knapdale branch soon attained to considerable power and influence. Their Chief was Macmillan of Knap, a person of acknowledged importance in the district. Through course of time the Knap family became extinct, and the chiefship went to Macmillan of Dunmore, an estate lying on the south side of Loch Tarbert. Duncan Macmillan of Dunmore had Arms registered in 1742, and he is described as "representative of the ancient family of Macmillan of Knap." After a while this branch also died out, when the MacNeills, by right of their intermarriage with the Macmillans, claimed the property. They were opposed by the Campbells; but the dispute was amicably adjusted by the estate passing by purchase into the hands of Sir Archibald Campbell of Inverneil in 1775.

The Chief of Clan Macmillan is Matthew Macmillan, Esq.

The Macmillans of Galloway are a well-known branch of the clan.

In some parts of Argyllshire the Macmillans are known as "*Na Belich*"—the Bells.

There is a Clan Macmillan Society in Glasgow.

MACMILLAN.

THE CLAN MACNAB.

Badge :—Roebuckberry (Stone Bramble), *Rubus Saxatilis* ;
also Dearca fithich (Crowberry).

LIKE several other Highland clans, the Macnabs are of ecclesiastical origin. In Gaelic they are called "*Clann-an-Aba*"—Children of the Abbot—and are descended from the Abbots of Glendochart. The clan lands were situated at the side of Loch Tay, and stretched along the course of the Dochart to the head of Strathfillan. The residence of the Chief was at Kinnel, on the banks of the Dochart.

The Macnabs suffered much in the early decades of the fourteenth century. They took arms against Bruce, and after Bannockburn their estates were forfeited and granted by Bruce to his loyal supporters. In 1336 Gilbert Macnab made peace with King David II., and obtained a charter for the Barony of Bovain, in Glendochart.

In 1612 the sons of Macnab stormed the stronghold of the Neishes, and put all save two to the sword.

Iain Min, or Smooth John (VIII.), led the clan under Montrose in 1645. In 1745 the family of the Chief fought for the House of Hanover ; but the clan was " out " for the Stewarts under Acharn, Inchewen, and Dundurn. John Macnab (XI.) died in 1788, and Francis became twelfth Chief. On his death, at Callander, in 1815, his nephew, Archibald, son of Dr. Robert Macnab, became Chief. Owing to financial difficulties, Archibald (XIII.) was obliged to sell his estates. He went to Canada in 1821, but returned in 1853. He died in France in 1860, aged eighty-three. He was survived by a widow and one daughter, out of a family of eight. His daughter, Sophia Frances, died at Florence in 1894.

A family of Macnabs were, for a period of four hundred years, hereditary armourers and jewellers to the Campbells of Loch Awe, whose seat was at Kilchurn Castle.

There is a Clan Society, with its headquarters in Edinburgh.

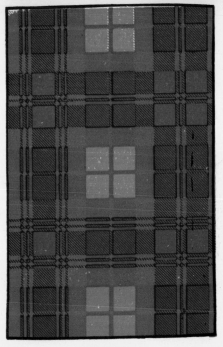

MACNAB.

THE CLAN MACNAUGHTON.

War Cry :—" Fraoch Eilean " (" The Heathery Isle," Loch Awe).
Badge :—Lus Albanach (Trailing Azalea).

THE earliest authentic reference to the Clan MacNaughton
connects them with Strathtay and Argyllshire. The
name Nectan is Pictish, and in the twelfth century the
Clan MacNaughton were proprietors of Strathtay, and were
styled *Tòiseachs* or Thanes of Lochtay. In the thirteenth
century we find them possessing land in Argyllshire. These
possessions extended over the upper part of Lochawe, Glenara,
Glenshira, and Loch Fyne. Their strongholds were " Fraoch
Eilean " Castle, Loch Awe, Castle " Dubh-Loch " in Glenshira,
and the more modern Castle of Dundarave on Loch Fyne.

Alexander III. in 1267 granted to *Gillichrist MacNachdan*
the keeping of his castle of *Fraoch Eilean* (Heathery Isle), Loch
Awe, so that they should cause it to be built and repaired at the
King's expense, as often as needful, and keep it safely for the
King's necessity ; and that as often as he should come to it,
the castle, well furnished, should be delivered to him to lodge
and dwell there at his pleasure. Between the years 1390 and
1406 Robert III. confirmed Maurice MacNaughtane a grant by
Colin Campbell of Lochow, in heritage, of various lands in
Over-Lochow.

In 1691 the MacNaughton estates were forfeited. The last
of the MacNaughtons of Dundarave was John, who married
about 1700 a daughter of Sir James Campbell, the last of the
Campbells of Ardkinglass in the direct male line. It is said
that Ardkinglass, Laban-like, deceived MacNaughton, who
found himself married to the eldest daughter instead of the
second. Local tradition says that the following day Mac-
Naughton and the second daughter fled to Ireland, leaving
his wife lamenting.

MACNAUGHTON.

THE MACNEILLS OF BARRA.

War Cry :—" Buaidh no Bàs " (" Victory or Death ").
Badge :—Machall-monaidh (Dryas) or Feamainn (Algæ).

IT is generally admitted that the MacNeills of Barra and
the MacNeills of Gigha have had a common origin. They
both trace themselves back to Neil Og, who flourished
about 1300. He was succeeded by his son, also Neil Og, who
is said to have been present at Bannockburn (1314), and to have
obtained a charter of the lands of Kintyre from Robert the
Bruce. Neil Og's grandson, Roderick, was succeeded by his
son, Gilleonan, who received a charter of the island of Barra
and the lands of Boisdale in South Uist in 1427. In 1688
Roderick MacNeill (XIV.) of Barra obtained a Crown charter
of Barra. Barra had to be parted with in 1840, when it was
sold to Colonel John Gordon of Cluny. The present (forty-
fifth) Chief is Robert Lister MacNeill of Barra, of Castlebay,
Barra, Inverness-shire.

The MacNeills of Gigha have always been regarded as the
oldest cadet family of the MacNeills of Barra. The Chief of
the MacNeills of Gigha in the first half of the sixteenth
century was Neil MacNeill. He had two sons—Neil, ancestor
of the MacNeills of Taynish, and John Og, ancestor of the
MacNeills of Gallachoille and of Crerar, afterwards of Colonsay. In 1554 Gigha was sold to James MacDonald of Islay.
In 1590 Hector MacNeill of Taynish purchased Gigha from
John Campbell of Calder, who had acquired it from MacDonald
of Islay. The estates of Gigha and Taynish were possessed
by his descendants till 1780, when the former was sold to
Alexander MacNeill of Colonsay, a cadet of the family. On
the death of Sir John Carstairs MacNeill, V.C., K.C.B., in
1904, Colonsay was sold to Lord Strathcona.

The MacNeills, a celebrated race of bards, were hereditary
harpers to the Macleans of Duart.

MACNEILL.

THE CLAN MACPHERSON.

War Cry :—" Creag Dhubh Chloinn Chatain " (" The
Black Craig of Clan Chattan ").
Badge :—Bocsa (Boxwood) or Lus nan cnàimhseag
(Red Whortleberry).

THE clan, as the name indicates, is of ecclesiastical origin.
The name Macpherson—Son of the Parson—was common
over the Highlands in the fifteenth and sixteenth
centuries.

Kenneth, the ancestor of Cluny, is mentioned in the Kinrara MSS. as contemporary with the Mackintosh Chief who
died in 1407; and Kenneth's son, Duncan Parsoun, married
this Chief's grand-daughter. From Duncan Parsoun, son of
Kenneth, both Skene and the Kinrara MS. trace the Cluny
family—for Duncan Parsoun is mentioned in 1438 as having
been prisoner in Tantallon Castle along with Alexander, Earl
of Ross (*Celtic Scot.*, III., 297–364). Kinrara makes Duncan
Parson of Laggan; but the Parson seems to have sprung from
the Strathnairn district, where his descendants held property
earliest of any Macphersons attached to Clan Chattan. The
genealogy from Duncan Parson runs thus : He was father of
Donald Mor and Bean, ancestor of Brin; Donald Mor was
ancestor of Donald Dall, who was father of Donald Og (died
1362), father of Ewen, father of Andrew *in* Cluny and *of* Grange,
in Banffshire. Andrew is a historical personage. He signs the
Macpherson Bond to Huntly in 1591, is tenant in Cluny in 1603
in the Gordon Rental (for " three pleuches "), and signs the
Clan Chattan Bond in 1609, as head of the Brin family.

The real Badenoch Macphersons are descended from Muir-
each Parson, and hence they are called *Clann Mhuirich*. The
Macphersons were among the best of Prince Charles's army.
Ewen remained in Badenoch in hiding for nine years after
Culloden, escaping to France in 1755, where he died next year.

MACPHERSON.

HUNTING MACPHERSON

THE Macphersons, like the MacLeods, have quite a number of settings of tartan associated with them. They are not all old, however, and several of them have no better authority than that they appear in the *Vestiarium Scoticum* (1842).

Commenting on the fact that the Macphersons had so many different settings, a representative of a Highland family who lived in the second half of the eighteenth century, writes : " When the Stewart princes published their *Vestiarium Scoticum*, Cluny was their friend, and they gave him five or six different tartans all to himself—the Cluny tartan, the Hunting tartan, the Dress tartan, etc."

The Cluny, or Full Dress tartan, is not older than the *Vestiarium*, which, though not published till 1842, was ready for the Press in 1829. Sir Thomas Dick Lauder, writing to Sir Walter Scott on 1st June 1829, says : " Cluny Macpherson appeared at the late fancy ball at Edinburgh in his beautiful and genuine tartan, as taken from the MS. (*Vestiarium*), which excited universal admiration."

What is now called the Macpherson Hunting tartan is found in the earliest collections, and it is more than likely that it was the pattern generally worn by the clan down to the middle of the last century, when the white ground was exchanged for grey.

The present Chief of the Clan Macpherson is Albert Cameron Macpherson (Cluny Macpherson) of Macpherson, Inverness-shire, Cluny Castle, Kingussie.

MACPHERSON, HUNTING.

THE CLAN MACQUARRIE.

War Cry:—" An t-Arm Breac Dearg " (" The Army of the
Checkered Red " [tartan]).
Badge:—Giuthas (Pine Tree).

THE name Macquarrie comes from the Gaelic *Guaire*, which
means noble. The Macquarries first appear in possession
of Ulva and part of Mull, and, like the Mackinnons,
" their situation forced them," says Skene, " to become de-
pendent upon the MacDonalds."

John Macquarrie of Ulva is the first on record, dying about
1473. After the forfeiture of the Lord of the Isles they followed Maclean of Duart. When, in 1609, the Bishop of the
Isles went to Iona as Commissioner for King James VI., among
the chief men of the Isles who submitted themselves to him
were Macquarrie of Ulva, Mackinnon of that Ilk, and ten
others.

Lachlan Macquarrie (XVI.) of Ulva was obliged to dispose
of his property, and in 1778, at the age of sixty-three, he
entered the army.

When the old 74th Regiment, or Argyll Highlanders, were
raised in 1777 by Colonel Campbell of Barbreck, Lachlan Macquarrie obtained a commission in it, and his name, under date
23rd December 1777, appears among the officers of this regiment, which was disbanded in 1783; and after a long life, the
last of the Macquarries of Ulva died in 1818 without male
issue, so his line is extinct. This Lachlan was the proprietor
of Ulva at the time of the visit of Dr. Johnson and Mr. Boswell
to that island in 1773.

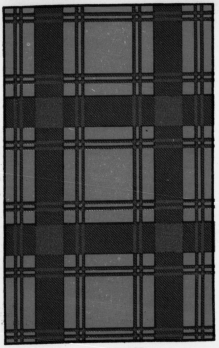

MACQUARRIE.

THE MACQUEENS.

Badge :—Bocsa (Boxwood) or Lus nan cnàimhseag, Braoileag
(Red Whortleberry).

THE Macqueens are of Norse origin, from Sweyn or Swyne,
rendered in Gaelic *MacCuine, MacShuibhne*. A Sween
Macqueen signs the Clan Chattan Bond of 1609. Although latterly regarded as a sept of the Clan Chattan, they
are more likely to be of Clan Ranald origin. In the thirteenth
century a family of MacSweens held lands in Kintyre, especially Castle Sween. In Skye we find the Gaelic name *MacSuain*
taking the form MacSween, MacSwan, and Swan in English.

Although originally but an offshoot of the Hebridean Macqueens who owed allegiance to the Lord of the Isles, the Macqueens of Corrybrough, who settled in Strathdearn, may be
said to have occupied the position of "head of the haill name."

The Macqueens are known as Clan Revan, and the circum-
stances under which the Macqueens left the West Coast and
settled in Strathdearn are stated to be as follows : Early in the
fifteenth century Malcolm Beg Mackintosh (tenth of Mackintosh)
married Mora MacDonald of Moidart, and with the bride came,
as was the custom, several of her kinsmen, who took up their
abode near her new home. Among the followers were Revan-
MacMulmor MacAngus, of whom the Clan Revan are descended,
and Donald Mac-Gillandrish, of whom the Clan Andrish.
Roderick Du Revan Macqueen is said to have fought under
Mackintosh at the battle of Harlaw, 1411.

On the death of John Fraser Macqueen in 1881, the succession to the chiefship, but not to the estate, opened to his only
surviving brother, Lachlan, a distinguished officer in the East
India Company, who died in 1896. He was succeeded in the
chiefship by his only son, Donald, now resident in New
Zealand.

MACQUEEN.

THE CLAN MACRAE.

War Cry :—" Sgùr Urain " (A mountain in Kintail).
Badge :—Garbhag an t-slèibhe (Fir Club Moss).

IT is generally understood that the name Macrae—Gaelic *MacRath*—means " Son of Grace," and had, in all probability, an ecclesiastical origin. It occurs as a personal or Christian name in Ireland, and also in Scotland, from the fifth to the thirteenth century. It was common as a surname in Galloway, Ayrshire, and the south of Perthshire in the fifteenth and sixteenth centuries, and is still common, with various forms of spelling—M'Crae, M'Crea, M'Creath, etc. In Ireland it takes the form Magrath.

The home of the Highland Clan Macrae, sometimes called " the Wild Macraes," was Kintail, in Ross-shire, where they are said to have migrated from the Lovat country about the middle of the fourteenth century. They were related to the MacKenzie Barons of Kintail, whose ablest and most loyal supporters they soon proved, and so became largely the means of raising the Barony of Kintail, afterwards the Earldom of Seaforth, to the high position it occupies in the annals of Scottish history. The Macraes were Chamberlains of Kintail for many generations, and frequently Vicars of the parish and Constables of Ellandonan Castle. The present Constable of Eilean-Donan Castle is Lieut.-Colonel John Macrae-Gilstrap.

Rev. Farquhar Macrae (1580-1662) was Vicar of Kintail for forty-four years. One of his sons, Rev. John Macrae of Dingwall (1614-1673), who took a prominent part in the ecclesiastical controversies of the time, was progenitor of the Macraes of Conchra, a family that has been honourably represented in the British army for several generations.

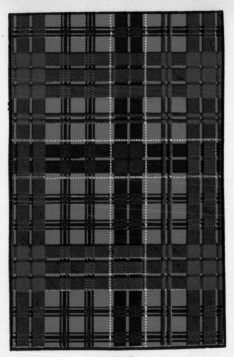

MACRAE.

THE CLAN MATHESON.

War Cry :—" Achadh-dà-thearnaidh " (" Field of the Two
Declivities ").

THE name Matheson is English in form; indeed, it applied
to the Lowland and English Mathewsons originally, and
common spellings of it were Mathieson and Matthison,
derived from Matthew. But the Highland clan was called in
Gaelic *Mac-mhathan* or *Mac-mhagan*, Son of the Bear (*math-
ghamhain*)—a common name in old Gaelic times, and equally
a favourite with Norse as Björn or Bjarni. The Irish form is
Macmahon.

The Mathesons appear in history earlier than their neighbours of Kintail. Kermac Macmaghan assisted the Earl of
Ross in 1262–63 against the Norse, especially in Skye.

All the Matheson genealogies converge in Murdoch Buidhe
ten generations back (in most cases) from the present day.

Sir Kenneth Matheson is descended from Dugall Matheson
of Balmacarra, second son of Murdoch Buidhe and Chamberlain
of Lochalsh.

A strong sept of Mathesons existed in Sutherland, east of
the " Cat " range, from 1492 downwards. They were no doubt
a sept of the Lochalsh family, as tradition holds. The chief
family had its seat at Shinness. In the Jacobite days Neil
Matheson was head of the Shinness family. From this family
descended Sir James Sutherland Matheson of the Lewis (1796-
1887). The present representative of the family is Lieut.-
Colonel Duncan Matheson of Achany.

It is generally understood that the chiefship of the clan now
lies with the representative of the Mathesons of Bennetsfield.

MATHESON.

THE CLAN MENZIES.

War Cry :—" Geal is Dearg a suas " (" Up with the White
and Red ").
Badge :—Uinnseann (Ash).

IT is generally believed that this clan is descended from a
Gaelic-speaking race, though the Chiefs are of Lowland
origin. The clan seems to have been settled in Athole
from an early period. The name occurs in charters during the
reign of William the Lion and the reign of Alexander II., for
we find that about that time Robert de Meyners grants a charter
of the lands of Culdares, in Fortingall, to Matthew de Mon-
crief. Sir Robert's son, Alexander, was possessor of the lands
of Weem, Aberfeldy, and Fortingall, in Athole, Glendochart
in Breadalbane, as well as Durisdeer in Nithsdale. From
Alexander's eldest son descended Sir Robert de Mengues,
Knight, whose lands were erected into the Barony of Menzies
in 1487. His descendant, Alexander Menzies of Castle Menzies,
was in 1665 created a Baronet of Nova Scotia.

A distinguished cadet family of the Menzieses was that of
Pitfoddels, who branched off from the main stock in the fourteenth century. The family is now extinct.

In the Rising of " the '45 " the Chief of the clan took no
part, though the clan was " out " under Menzies of Shian.

To a Menzies Scotland is indebted for the introduction of
the larch tree, which now flourishes all over the Highlands.
The first larch saplings planted in Scotland were raised from
seven seedlings brought in 1738 from the Tyrol by Menzies of
Culdares.

There is a Clan Menzies Society in Glasgow.

MENZIES.

THE CLAN MORRISON.

War Cry :—" Dun Eistein " (A fort in Lewis).
Badge :—Sgòd cladaich (Driftwood).

AS a Highland clan the Morrisons belong to Lewis and the
adjoining mainland of North-West Scotland. The Morrisons of Perth and Lennox formed no clan, and the name
in Gaelic is different. The latter is from Maurice, Gaelic
Moiris.

The Clan Morrison derive their name from an adaptation
of Gaelic *MacGille-mhoire* or *M'Gilmor*, *Gille-mhoire* meaning
" Devotee of St. Mary." John Morisone, " indweller " of Lewis,
writing about 1680, records that the first inhabitants of Lewis
were then men of three races—Mores, son of Kennanus Makurich, son of a King of Norway ; Iskair MacAulay, an Irishman (Issachar or Zachary MacAulay) ; and MacNicol, whose
only daughter married Claudius, son of Olave, King of Norway.
This, it will be seen, accounts for the three original clans of
Lewis—MacLeods, MacAulays, and Morrisons. The MacLeods
were undoubtedly of Norse origin. The English form Morrison
goes as far back as the sixteenth century.

The first recorded Morrison is Hugh or Hucheon (Gaelic,
Uisdean), the Brieve, contemporary of practically the last
MacLeod of Lewis, Roderick MacLeod, Chief from about
1532-1595. The Brieve held the hereditary office of deemster
—judge or " law man," as the Norse called them. The
Morrisons are still an important clan in the Hebrides and in the
north-west mainland of Scotland.

Mr. Hugh Morrison of Islay is married to a daughter of the
late Earl Granville and a grand-daughter of the late W. F.
Campbell of Shawfield and Islay.

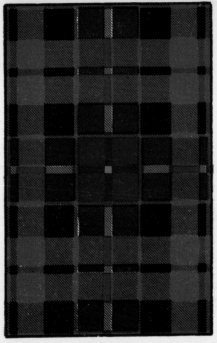

MORRISON.

THE CLAN MUNRO.

War Cry :—" Caisteal Fólais 'na theine " (" Castle Foulis ablaze ").
Badge :—Garbhag nan Gleann (Common Club Moss).

THE surname Munro seems to be from a place-name, as the first Chiefs in the fourteenth century are called *de Munro*. In Gaelic they are called *Clann Rothaich*. The first assured Chief by charter evidence is Robert de Munro (1341–72).

In 1544 and 1550 two bonds of Kindness and Alliance were signed between Ross of Balnagowan and Robert Munro of Foulis.

Robert, the eighteenth Chief, went over to Sweden with Sir Donald Mackay, first Lord Reay, in 1626, and joined the army of Gustavus Adolphus. He died in 1633, and was succeeded by his brother, Hector, who in 1634 was created by Charles I. a Baronet of Nova Scotia. On the death of Sir Hector's son and heir the direct line of the chiefs became extinct. The title and property then passed to Robert Munro of Opisdale, grandson of George, third son of the fifteenth Chief of Foulis.

In 1740, when the independent companies of the Black Watch were formed into the 43rd (afterwards 42nd) Regiment, Sir Robert Munro, sixth Baronet, had the honour of being appointed its Lieutenant-Colonel, John, Earl of Crawford, being the Colonel. Sir Robert's next brother, George, was one of the Captains, while his youngest brother, James, became surgeon of the regiment.

The present Chief of the Munroes is Sir Hector, eleventh Baronet, Hon. Colonel and late Colonel commanding 3rd Battalion Seaforth Highlanders. The residence of the Chief is Foulis Castle.

MUNRO.

MURRAY OF ATHOLE.

Badge :—Calg-bhealaidh (Butchers' Broom) or Aitionn (Juniper).

TRADITION ascribes the descent of the Murrays to Freskin, a Fleming, who settled in Scotland during the reign of King David I., and who acquired a grant of land in Moray. He was succeeded by his elder son, William, who was, in turn, succeeded by his son, William, who assumed the designation of " De Moravia," in consequence of his large territorial possessions in the province of Moray. This William de Moravia had, besides his heir, Sir Walter, left several other sons, from one of whom are descended the Murrays of Tullibardine, progenitors of the Dukes of Athole and Chiefs of the Clan Murray of Athole. (*See* Murray of Tullibardine.)

William, second Earl of Tullibardine, married Lady Dorothea Stewart, eldest daughter and heir-of-line of the fifth Earl of Athole (of the first Stewart creation), who died in 1594 without male issue. His son, John, as heir-of-line of the Stewart Earls of Athole, was in 1629 created by King Charles I. the first Earl of Athole of the Murray line. The second Earl was raised to the dignity of Marquis of Athole, while the third Earl and second Marquis became in 1703 Duke of Athole.

The second Duke of Athole, in right of his mother, succeeded to the Sovereignty of the Isle of Man. These rights the third Duke ceded in 1765 for a money compensation.

President Forbes, writing to the Government in 1745, says : " The Murrays is no clan family, though the Duke of Athole is Chief and head of a number of barons and gentlemen of the name of Murray in the Lowlands."

The present Duke is the eighth holder of that title. His seat is Blair Castle, Perthshire.

MURRAY OF ATHOLE.

MURRAY OF TULLIBARDINE.

Badge :—Calg-bhealaidh (Butchers' Broom) or Aitionn (Juniper).

THE Murrays of Tullibardine are progenitors of the Dukes of Athole and Chiefs of the Clan Murray of Athole (*see* Murray, Athole). Though that is so, their representative is not the head of the Murray family. Two other branches have a prior claim to the headship of the family, viz. : The Murrays of Polmaise and the Moray-Stirlings of Abercairney and Ardoch. The latter family became extinct in the male line in 1859. The Murrays of Touchadam and Polmaise and the Murrays of Abercairney were lineally descended from Sir Walter, eldest son of William de Moravia. While, therefore, the Duke of Athole is *Chief* of the Clan Murray of Athole, the *head* of the Murray *family* would appear to be Murray of Polmaise. The Murrays of Tullibardine, Dukes of Athole and Chiefs of the Murrays of Athole, are descended from a younger son of William de Moravia, grandson of Freskin, the progenitor of the Murrays.

Sir John Murray, the twelfth feudal Baron of Tullibardine, was by James VI. in 1606 created Earl of Tullibardine.

The Marquis of Tullibardine having, with his two brothers, been " out " in 1715, was attainted for his share in that Rising. He consequently did not succeed to the Dukedom of Athole on the death of his father ; the family honours therefore passed to his immediate younger brother, James, who became the second Duke of Athole. The attainted Marquis of Tullibardine and his talented brother, Lord George Murray, took a prominent part in the Rising of 1745. It was the Marquis who unfurled Prince Charles's standard in Glenfinnan, while Lord George Murray was commander of the Prince's forces.

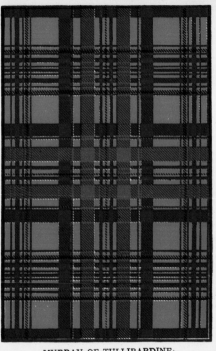

MURRAY OF TULLIBARDINE.

THE CLAN OGILVIE.

Badge :—Sgitheach geal (Whitethorn, Hawthorn).

THIS clan derives its origin from one Gillebride, second son of Gillechrist, Earl of Angus. Gillebride assumed the name of his property, which was the Barony of Ogilvie in the parish of Glamis, Forfarshire, granted to him by William the Lion about 1163.

Patrick de Ogilvie figures in the Ragman Roll. He left two sons, both adherents of Robert the Bruce. Sir Patrick obtained for his services lands in Forfarshire. Sir Walter, a descendant of Sir Patrick, was succeeded by his son, Alexander, whose sole issue was a daughter. On the death of Sir Alexander, the chiefship of the clan passed to his younger brother, Sir Walter. Sir John, eighth Baron, obtained in 1458 a charter of the lands of Airlie. His son, Sir James, was in 1491 elevated to the Peerage as Lord Ogilvie of Airlie. James, eighth Lord Ogilvie, was created Earl of Airlie by Charles I. in 1639.

During all the troubles of the House of Stewart, the Ogilvies of Airlie stood loyally by the ancient monarchy. For this they suffered much. Several representatives of the family were attainted for the part they took in the Risings of 1715 and 1745. In 1778 a pardon was granted to Lord Ogilvie, in consideration of his extreme youth at the time of 1745—he was but twenty-one at the time ; the Earldom of Airlie was at the same time revived, and the estates to a certain extent restored. The seat of the Airlie family is Cortachy Castle, on the river South Esk.

The ninth and present Earl of Airlie is David Lyulph Gore Wolseley Ogilvie, K.C.V.O., M.C.

L OGILVIE.

THE ROBERTSONS
(OR CLANN DONNACHAIDH).

Badge :—Dlùth Fhraoch (Fine-leaved Heath) or An Raineach
mhór (Bracken).

THE first Chief of this clan was *Donnachadh Reamhar*
(Duncan the Stout)—hence the designation *Clann
Donnachaidh*, or Children of Duncan. This Duncan was
the male descendant and representative of the ancient Celtic
Earls of Athole.

" The Robertsons of Struan," says Skene, " are unquestion-
ably the oldest family in Scotland, being the sole remaining
branch of that Royal House which occupied the throne of
Scotland during the eleventh and twelfth centuries."

In later centuries Clann Donnachaidh and its Chiefs were
noted for their intense loyalty to the Stewarts.

When the clan lands were erected into the Barony of Struan,
the Chief's name was Robert, and his son took the name of
Robertson, which became thereafter that of the family and
clan.

In ancient days the Chiefs had castles in Rannoch and at
Invervack, near Struan ; later, and up to about 1860, their
principal residence was Dunalastair, or Mount Alexander,
magnificently situated at the foot of, and in full view of,
Shiehallion, in Rannoch ; other residences were Carie, Dall,
and Rannoch Barracks. The burial-places are at Struan and
Dunalastair.

Miss Jean Rosine Robertson in 1910 succeeded as head of
the clan her brother, Alasdair Stewart Robertson (twentieth
from *Donnachadh Reamhar*), and still owns the estate of
Rannoch Barracks, at the extreme west end of Loch Rannoch,
on which is some of the finest fishing in the Highlands. The
Barracks was originally built for the troops stationed there
after " the '45," but was afterwards converted into a residence.

The oldest cadet family of Struan were the Robertsons of
Lude ; others are the Robertsons of Inshes, Kindeace, Auch-
leeks, Kindrochit, Strathloch, Ladykirk, Faskally, Blairfettie,
Killiehangy, and many other lairdships, chiefly in Athole and
the surrounding parts of Perthshire.

The Chief of the clan is styled Struan Robertson.

A Clan Society was formed in 1893.

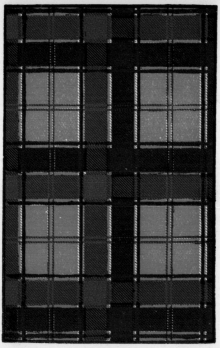

ROBERTSON.

THE ROB ROY TARTAN.

THERE are three portraits of Rob Roy MacGregor extant, all three taken from life, and each representing him dressed in this peculiar tartan. It is not improbable that the harsh and cruel proscription of his name, his clan, and his insignia, may have led to the adoption of this peculiar and neutral tartan by Rob Roy, the famous outlaw and Jacobite leader.

Robert MacGregor Campbell, which last name he bore repugnantly, in consequence of the Scottish Parliamentary Acts passed for the suppression of his clan, was a younger son of Lieutenant-Colonel MacGregor of Glengyle (an office in the Scottish army of James VII.), and his mother was a daughter of Campbell of Glenfalloch. Thus he was well born, but when is uncertain. He was certainly, however, active in the scenes of war and turbulence subsequent to the Revolution. "His own designation," says Sir Walter Scott, "was of Inversnaid; but he appears to have acquired a right of some kind or other to the property of Craig Royston, a domain of rock and forest lying on the east side of Loch Lomond, where that beautiful lake stretches into the dusky mountains of Glenfalloch."

For many years he maintained a predatory warfare against the Duke of Montrose, whose factor, Graham of Killearn, he made prisoner, and whose rents he drew on more than one occasion. He was married to Mary Helen MacGregor, daughter of MacGregor of Cromar, Loch Lomond side, and died 28th December 1734. His grave, and that of his wife, are still to be seen at the east end of the old ruined church at Balquhidder. He left four sons—Coll, Ronald, James, and Robert.

ROB ROY.

THE ROSES.

THE family of the Chief of this clan, Rose of Kilravock, settled in the county of Nairn in the reign of David I. ; but their first designation appears to have been " of Geddes," in the county of Inverness, Hugh Rose appearing as a witness to the foundation charter of the Priory of Beauly by Sir John Bisset of Lovat in 1219.

His son and successor, also Hugh, acquired the lands of Kilravock by his marriage with Mary, daughter of Sir Andrew de Bosco by Elizabeth, his wife (who was daughter and co-heiress of Sir John Bisset of Lovat). He was succeeded by his son, William, who married Morella, daughter of Alexander de Doun, by whom he had two sons — Andrew, the second, ancestor of the Roses of Auchlossan, in Mar ; and Hugh, his successor, who, in a deed of agreement respecting the Prior of Urquhart and the Vicar of Dalcross, is styled " nobilis vir Hugo Rose, dominus de Kilravock." His son, Hugh, married Janet, daughter of Sir Robert Chisholm, Constable of the Castle of Urquhart, by whom he received a large accession of lands in Strathnairn, etc.

The " Barons of Kilravock " intermarried with the first families in the North, and filled various situations of high trust and honour. The Castle is an old picturesque building, situated on the bank of the river Nairn. It is still inhabited, and contains some old armour, portraits, and family relics. There is scarcely any family whose charter chest is more amply stored with documents, not only of private importance, but of great antiquarian interest.

The seat of the Chief is still the Castle of Kilravock, which has been the residence of the Roses since 1460.

The present representative of the family is Lieutenant-Colonel Hugh Rose, C.M.G.

ROSE

THE CLAN ROSS.

THIS clan is known to Highlanders as *Clann Aindreas*—Sons of Andrew. It is generally admitted that the progenitor of the old Earls of Ross was the eldest son of *Gilleoin na h-Airde*, the ancestor of Anrias, who, again, was the progenitor of the O'Beolans or Gillanders, the old Celtic Earls of Ross. The first of the O'Beolan Earls of Ross was *Fearchar Mac-an-t-Sagairt* (Son of the Priest), hailing from Applecross. For services rendered to Alexander II., Fearchar was knighted by the King, and in 1234 he was created Earl of Ross. The fifth Earl of Ross (William) died in 1372, leaving no sons. On his death the chiefship passed to Hugh of Rariches, his brother. Hugh was the progenitor of the Rosses of Balnagowan. At the beginning of the eighteenth century David Ross of Balnagowan was the last of his race in the direct line. He therefore disposed of the estate to General Charles Ross, brother of Lord Ross of Hawkhead, a family which, however, was in nowise related to his own. Upon the death, in 1711, of David, the last Ross of Balnagowan, the lineal male representation of the O'Beolan Rosses became vested in the Munro Rosses of Pitcalnie.

The obituary notices for August 1884 contain the death of "Mr. George Ross of Pitcalnie, in Ross-shire, and Arnot, in Kincardine, aged eighty-one. Deceased was the last representative of the ancient Earls of Ross, and was Chief of the Clan Ross." He was succeeded by a grand-nephew.

In 1745 the fighting force of the clan was 500 men.

The surname Ross is from the county name *Ros*, so named from *ros*, the Gaelic for promontory.

ROSS.

SCOTT.

War Cry :—" A Bellendaine ! "

UCHTREDUS filius Scoti lived in 1130. He was father of
Richard, who is said to have had two sons—Richard,
ancestor of the Scotts of Buccleuch, and Sir Michael,
ancestor of the Scotts of Balweary. From Richard, the eldest
son, descended Sir Richard, who married the heiress of Mur-
thockstone, and died 1320, leaving a son, Michael, father of two
sons, Robert and Walter of Synton. Robert's great-grandson
was Sir Walter, who had two sons—Sir David of Branxholm and
Alexander of Howpaisley. Sir David had two sons : (1) David,
whose great-great-grandson, Sir Walter, was created Baron Scott
of Buccleuch, 1606 ; and (2) Robert, ancestor of the Scotts of
Scotstarvit. The first Lord Scott died in 1611, and was succeeded by his son, Walter, who was created Earl of Buccleuch,
1619. On the death of Mary, daughter of Francis, second Earl,
the title went to her sister, Anne, Countess of Buccleuch, who
married James, Duke of Monmouth. On their marriage they
were created Duke and Duchess of Buccleuch, 1673.

Sir Michael Scott of Balweary was great-grandfather of
another Sir Michael, who was known as the wizard. Sir
William Scott, seventh Baronet of Ancrum, died in 1902, when
the Baronetcy became extinct (or dormant).

Bellendean, near the head of the Borthwick Water in Roxburghshire, was the gathering-place of the Clan Scott in times
of war ; for which purpose it was very convenient, being in
the centre of the possessions of the Chiefs of this name. " A
Bellendaine ! " is accordingly cited in old ballad books as their
gathering word or war cry.

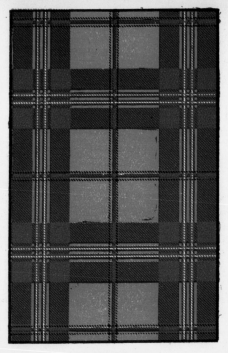

SCOTT.

THE SINCLAIRS.

Badge :—Conasg (Whin or Gorse).

THE Sinclairs are not, strictly speaking, a Highland clan. The founder of the family was Comte de Sancto Claro, who accompanied William the Conqueror to England. William, son of the Comte, settled in Scotland in the reign of King David I., and obtained from that monarch a grant of the Barony of Roslin. Sir Henry de Sancto Claro, his descendant, was a constant supporter of King Robert the Bruce. Sir William, the grandson of Sir Henry, laid the foundation of the Northern family of Sinclairs by marrying one of the daughters and co-heiresses of Malise, Earl of Strathearn, Caithness, and Orkney. The eldest son of this marriage, Henry Sinclair of Roslin, was recognised as Earl of Orkney. William, third *Sinclair* Earl of Orkney, received in 1455 a grant of the Earldom of Caithness. The direct line of Sinclair Earls of Caithness came to an end with the death, in 1676, of George, sixth Earl.

The Sinclairs of the West, especially of Argyllshire, do not seem to have any connection with the Sinclairs of Caithness. In the West they are called in Gaelic *Clann-na-Cearda*—Children of the Craft, or Craftsmen. The general name for craftsman, or gold and tinsmith, was in Gaelic *ceàrd*, whence the surname Caird. Records and documents of the fifteenth and sixteenth centuries abound with the name M'Nacaird (Glenlochy, 1590), M'Necaird, and M'Nokerd (*Black Book of Taymouth*, 1594-1621). In Islay M'Nokard, M'Nakard (1688, 1733). In Islay and Argyll generally it still exists as *Mac-na-Cearda*, and this is Englished by the Norman name of Sinclair.

The Earl of Caithness is the Chief of Clan Sinclair.

SINCLAIR.

SKENE.

THE progenitor of the Skenes is generally understood to have been a younger son of Robertson of Struan. During a Royal hunting expedition to the forest of Socket, Aberdeenshire, King Malcolm Canmore was attacked by a large wolf, whereupon young Robertson with his *sgian* or dirk killed the animal. As a reward for this brave deed Robertson was rewarded with the Barony of Skene, in Aberdeenshire. The above tradition seems to be confirmed by the armorial bearings of the Skenes, who, by the way, are known in Gaelic as *Siol Sgeine, no Clann Donnachaidh Mhàr*. The family Arms are : Gules, three dirks or *skenes* supported by three wolves' heads ; Crest—an arm holding a garland ; Supporters—two Highlandmen ; Motto—" *Virtatis regia merces.*"

In 1318 King Robert I., by charter, granted to his beloved and faithful Robert Skene the lands and loch of Skene.

The family of Skene of Skene became extinct in the direct line in 1827, when the estates of the family devolved on James, fourth Earl of Fife, nephew of the last Skene of Skene. The male representation of the Skenes seems to have passed to the family of Skene of Halyards, descended from Andrew of Anchorie, second son of James Skene, twelfth Chief, who died in 1605. The chiefship of the Skenes would now appear to be vested in the family of Prerau, in Austria, whose progenitor was Patrick, second son of Andrew Skene of Anchorie.

Among the notable Scotsmen of the nineteenth century William Forbes Skene will hold a foremost place. He was born in Kincardineshire in 1809, and died in Edinburgh in 1893. He was the author of *Celtic Scotland* (3 Vols.), *The Highlanders of Scotland, The Four Ancient Books of Wales* (2 Vols.), and *Chronicles of the Picts and Scots.* In 1881 he was appointed Historiographer-Royal for Scotland.

SKENE.

THE ROYAL STEWARTS.

Badge :—Darag (Oak) or Cluaran (Thistle), the present
National badge.

THE ancestor of this gallant and Royal race was a Breton
noble, Alan, a cadet of the ancient Counts of Dol and
Dinan, in Brittany. Crossing to England, he was appointed Sheriff of Shropshire by Henry I., and by his third
son, Walter Fitz-Alan, was progenitor of the House of Stewart.
Walter crossed the Border, and received from King David I.
the office of Great Steward of Scotland, an office subsequently
made hereditary in the family.

Walter, the third Stewart, assumed as his family surname
the name of his office.

Walter, the sixth Stewart, at the age of twenty-one led his
vassals to Bannockburn. The following year he married the
Princess Marjory Bruce, by whom he had one son, Robert, who
ultimately ascended the throne as Robert II. He left a numerous family of sons, but there is now no single legitimate male
descendant of any of the Stewart Kings. The direct male line
absolutely failed with James V., whose daughter, Mary, married
Henry, Lord Darnley, who, singularly enough, was the senior
male representative of the Bonkyl branch, and by this union
their son, James VI., was thus not only the heir male (through
his father) of the High Stewards of Scotland, but also heir-of-
line (through his mother) of the main stem. Male descendants
again failed on the death of Prince Charlie and his brother,
the Duke of York.

There is a Stewart Society in Edinburgh.

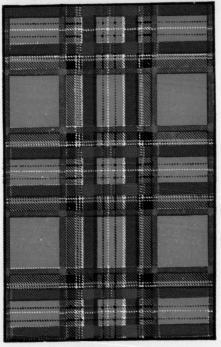

STEWART, ROYAL.

THE DRESS STEWART.

THIS tartan has been named, but on what authority it is uncertain, the "Dress Stewart," which it certainly is not now, the Royal red tartan being that used on dress or ceremonial occasions, while "the Old Hunting," etc., tartans are most used on ordinary occasions. Charles II. is said to have sometimes worn shoulder knots of a tartan similar to this, which may have occasioned the name. It owes its prominence as a Stewart tartan to-day to the favour of Her late Majesty, Queen Victoria.

James VI. of Scotland and I. of England left, with other children, a daughter, Elizabeth, who married Frederick V., Duke of Bavaria, Elector Palatine of the Rhine. His youngest daughter, Sophia, married in 1658 Ernest Augustus, Duke of Brunswick-Lunenburgh, Elector of Hanover. The son of the Elector, George Lewis, became King of Great Britain and Ireland as George I., and died in 1727, leaving behind him a son, afterwards George II. He was succeeded by his grandson, George III., who left thirteen children, two of whom succeeded to the throne under the titles of George IV. and William IV. The fourth son of George III., Edward, Duke of Kent, married in 1818 Victoria Mary Louisa, daughter of His Serene Highness, Francis, Duke of Saxe-Coburg-Saalfield. His daughter, Alexandrina Victoria, on the death of her uncle, William IV., ascended the throne on the 30th June 1837 as Queen Victoria. His present Majesty, King George V., is now the representative of this branch of the Stewarts.

STEWART, DRESS.

HUNTING STEWART.

ALTHOUGH it seems impossible to trace the history of this tartan or fix the date of its introduction, as it has long been a favourite with the people of Scotland, we thought it right to preserve in this work a record of one of the most beautiful tartans associated with the Stewarts. Hunting tartans were not unusual with the more important families, the object being to have a design which would harmonise more closely with the landscape than the ordinary Dress tartan. It is needless to say that the Stewart Kings, and, indeed all branches of the Stewarts, were keen sportsmen, devoted to hawk and hound. They had innumerable hunting forests and hunting seats, but the best known to-day is Castle Stalcaire (commonly spelt Stalker) in Appin, built by the Chief of Appin as a Royal residence for the Sovereign while hunting in Lorn.

In this connection it may be stated that the first indisputable reference to Highland tartan occurs in the *Accounts of the Lord High Treasurer of Scotland* in August 1538. These accounts contain the following items :—

"Item, in the first for ij elnis ane quarter elne of variant *cullorit velvet* to be the Kingis grace ane *schort Heland coit*, price of the elne vj. lib. ; summa XIIJ. lib. Xs.

"Item, for iij. elnis of *Heland Tartane* to be *hoiss* to the Kingis grace, price of the elne IIIJs. IIJd ; summa, XIIJs."

These articles formed part of the dress worn by James V. when hunting in the Highlands.

STEWART, HUNTING.

PRINCE CHARLES EDWARD.

Badge :—Darag (Oak) or Cluaran (Thistle).

THIS tartan, ever associated with "Bonnie Prince Charlie," is nowise different from the Royal Stewart, except that the broad red stripe in the former is very much contracted.

The achievements and adventures of the unfortunate Prince in the ever-memorable campaign of 1745-46 are too well known to be referred to at length. He was born at Rome 31st December 1720, he landed in Scotland 23rd July 1745, and on 19th August raised his father's standard in Glenfinnan, but was defeated at Culloden 16th April 1746. He died at Rome 31st January 1788. His funeral obsequies were celebrated in the cathedral of Frascati of which See his brother, the Cardinal Duke of York, was Bishop. The church was draped with black and gold lace and silver tissue, which, with the many wax lights, gave it a very solemn aspect. A large catafalque was erected on steps in the nave of the edifice, on which lay the Prince's coffin, covered by a superb pall whereon lay the Garter, St. George, and St. Andrew, which are now in the Castle of Edinburgh. It was embroidered with the Arms of Britain.

At 10 A.M. the old Cardinal came to the church in a sedan, and, seating himself at the altar, began in a broken voice to sing the office for the dead. "The first verse was scarcely finished when it was observed that his voice faltered, and tears trickled down his furrowed cheeks, so that it was feared he would not have been able to proceed ; however, he soon recollected himself, and went through the function in a very affecting manner, in which manly firmness, fraternal affection, and religious solemnity were happily blended."

So with that solemn scene ended many a century of stirring Scottish history.

STEWART, PRINCE CHARLES EDWARD.

THE STEWARTS OF APPIN.

War Cry :—" Creag an Sgairbh " (" The Cormorant's Rock "),
on which is built Caisteal an Stalcaire (Castle Stalker).
Badge :—Darag (Oak) or Cluaran (Thistle).

ALTHOUGH the term "clan" is sometimes applied to
Stewarts in general, only in regard to a branch—the
Stewarts of Appin—can it be appropriately used. The
other lines, Highland or Lowland, acted independently or
under the feudal chief of their district; the Appin Stewarts
alone had the characteristics of a Highland clan, being governed
on patriarchal lines following a hereditary chief.

Their ancestor was Sir James Stewart, third son of Sir John
Stewart, killed at Falkirk in 1298. Sir James Stewart fell at
Halidon Hill in 1333. On the forefeiture of the MacDougalls
of Lorn for adherence to the English interests, their Lordship
of Lorn passed with the hands of the two co-heiresses to the
two brothers, Sir John and Sir Robert Stewart.

On the death of Sir John Stewart, last Lord of Lorn, the
Lordship of Lorn passed to the Campbells. Sir John left three
daughters who each married a Campbell. He also had a son,
Dugald, by a lady of the Clan MacLaren, in Balquhidder.
Sir John married Dugald's mother, and from this Dugald are
descended the Stewarts of Appin. Dugald managed to secure
and maintain the district of Appin in Upper Lorn. After
Flodden the lands of Appin were parcelled out by the Chief—
Allan (III.) of Appin — amongst his sons, the ancestors
respectively of Appin, Strathgarry, Achnacone, Invernahyle,
and Fasnacloich. Of these, Achnacone alone retains his
paternal lands.

The present Chief of the clan is Robert Bruce Stewart,
Esquire, who is now designated "Stewart of Lorn, Appin, and
Ardshiel."

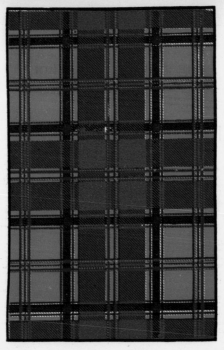

STEWART, APPIN.

THE STEWARTS OF ATHOLE.

Badge :—Darag (Oak) or Cluaran (Thistle).

THIS tartan is not to be confused with the dark green tartan commonly known as Athole tartan, which properly belongs to no family, but is purely a district or local tartan used by Athole men generally, particularly Stewarts and Robertsons, who formed the bulk of the population. The ancient Earldom of Athole was held by several of the Stewarts, notably Robert II., his son, Walter, and his ill-fated grandson, David, Duke of Rothesay. The title was ultimately conferred by James II. on his half-brother, Sir John Stewart of Balveny.

The Athole Stewarts were credited with a fighting strength of 1000 men, and reputed amongst the most disaffected to the Orange and Hanoverian successions. During the reign of William of Orange " 1500 Athole men as reputed for arms as any in the kingdom " joined the Marquis of Tullibardine to take part with Viscount Dundee but, on learning that Tullibardine designed to take the opposite side, they at once put themselves under the command of Stewart of Ballechin and set off to join Dundee's forces. In the subsequent battle of Killiecrankie they took a leading share. At Culloden, the Athole men and Camerons formed the right wing, and completely routed the Hanoverian regiments opposed to them.

The tartan here shown is believed to have been the distinctive tartan of these Athole Stewarts. It is copied from a Highland dress worn by a Stewart from Athole during " the '45," and still in the possession of a descendant.

STEWART, ATHOLE.

THE CLAN SUTHERLAND.

War Cry :—" Ceann na Drochaide Bige " (" The Head of the
Little Bridge "), a bridge at Dunrobin.
Badge :—Calg-bhealaidh (Butchers' Broom) or Canach
(Cotton Sedge).

THE surname Sutherland is derived from the Norse name
Sudrland—South Land—the country being south of
Caithness or *Gallaibh*, the Country of the Strangers.
The Chiefs of the clan are descended from Freskin, the progenitor of the Murrays. William de Moravia, Freskin's eldest
son, became the ancestor of the Murrays; while from a younger
son, Hugh, were derived the old Earls of Sutherland. This
Hugh received from King William the Lion the southern portions of Caithness in 1197. The first Earl of Sutherland is
understood to have been Walter, who received the Earldom
in 1061.

The last Earl of Sutherland, Chief of the clan, was Earl
John, who died in 1514, leaving no issue. He was succeeded
in the Earldom by his sister, Elizabeth, who had married
Adam Gordon of Aboyne, second son of the Earl of Huntly.
In 1766 the line of the Gordon Earls of Sutherland again
ended in a female, the Countess Elizabeth, who married
George Granville Leveson-Gower, Viscount Trentham, afterwards Marquis of Stafford. That nobleman was created Duke
of Sutherland in the Peerage of the United Kingdom. The
Countess Elizabeth held the Earldom for seventy-two years
and seven months, dying in 1839.

The fifth and present Duke of Sutherland is Sir George
Granville Sutherland-Leveson-Gower, K.T.

A Clan Sutherland Society was formed in Edinburgh in
1897.

SUTHERLAND.

THE CLAN URQUHART.

Badge :—Lus-leth-an-t-Samhraidh (Wallflower, Gillyflower).

THIS clan takes its name from the district so called in Ross-shire. The Urquharts of Cromarty were hereditary Sheriffs of the old county of Cromarty, nearly all of which originally belonged to them. We find certain charters dated at the castle of the Lord of Urquhart in 1342, and among the witnesses was one Adam de Urquhart.

In 1449 a Thomas Urquhart was Bishop of Ross; and the last Dean of Ross, in 1585, was Alexander Urquhart.

In the Roll of Landlords in 1587 John Urquhart of Craigfintry and Culbo appears as guardian to his grand-nephew, afterwards Sir Thomas Urquhart of Cromarty, father of the famous Knight of the same name.

In 1649 the Castle of Inverness was nearly demolished by Sir Thomas Urquhart of Cromarty and other cavaliers. He was one of the most quaint writers of the seventeenth century, and is chiefly known as the translator of Rabelais. Sir Thomas was author of several works. His poetic work, *Epigrams : Divine and Moral*, contains some good things, among the best being this on Woman :

> " Take *man* from *woman*, all that she can show
>   Of her own proper, is nought else but *wo*."

He was continually in monetary difficulties, and his estates were forfeited during Cromwell's rule. How and when he died is unknown. The Cromarty estates shortly after came into the hands of the MacKenzies, and now are a Peerage.

Major Beauchamp Colclough-Urquhart of Meldrum and Byth, Aberdeenshire, was head of the family, but he died as the result of wounds received at the battle of Atbara, 1898.

URQUHART.

KILTS
for Girls and Boys

Regulation Clan Tartan Kilts, with apron front, attached to white cotton bodice, with deep tuck for lengthening. In sizes 3 to 16 years. Girls, price, for the first size, **25/6**
Rising 2/- for each size.

Boys, heavier weight material 35/-
Rising 1/6 for each size.

Well – tailored Shirt Blouse, in Jap Silk or Tussore.   Price, for all sizes, **14/6**

Tartan Tie . . . . price **2/6**

179 Clan Tartans available. Full list and measurement form on request.

AUTHENTIC
CLAN TARTAN RUGS

Travelling Rugs in the Tartans of the principal Scottish clans can always be supplied from stock by Jenners.   Prices from
18/6

Bagpipe Makers   Highland Costume Outfitters   Established 1868

PETER HENDERSON LTD.

Bagpipe Makers and Highland Costumiers

24 RENFREW STREET, GLASGOW, C.2.

DRAMBUIE

Prince Charles Edward's Liqueur

This exquisite after-dinner Liqueur
is the finest that the British Empire
produces.   Made in the Isle of Skye
for nearly two centuries from a
recipe brought to Scotland by a
follower of Bonnie Prince Charlie
in 1745.

THE DRAMBUIE LIQUEUR COY. LTD.

8 & 9, UNION STREET, EDINBURGH

" LYDIA"—In plain stitch Pure Cashmere and Pure Wool. All fashionable colourings. Pleated or Flared skirt to match also obtainable.

"Pesco" Scottish Sportswear has a proud reputation amongst women of elegance on both sides of the Tweed. Its appeal is twofold. It has the excellent reliability of pure wool, knitted by Scottish craftspeople, and the charm of style which only Paris can evoke.

Pesco

SCOTTISH SPORTSWEAR

Obtainable from all high-class outfitters. In case of difficulty, write for illustrations of current Pesco models and names of nearest agents. Also Pesco Underwear, Bathing Suits, and Hosiery for Ladies, Gentlemen and Children.

PETER SCOTT & CO. LTD. (DEPT. SC), HAWICK, SCOTLAND